Cosmic Marriage

Reinhold Ebertin

Copyright 1974 by Ebertin-Verlag, Reinhold Ebertin.

All rights reserved.

No part of this book may be reproduced or transmitted in any form or by any means, electronic, mechanical, including photocopying or recording, or by any information storage and retrieval system, without written permission from the author and publisher, except in the case of a brief quotations embodied in critical reviews and articles. Requests and inquiries may be mailed to: American Federation of Astrologers, Inc., 6535 S. Rural Road, Tempe, Arizona, 85283.

Translated by Linda Kratzsch

First Printing in German 1937
Revised Edition in English 1974
Current Printing 2004

ISBN 0-86690-089-6

Published by:
American Federation of Astrologers, Inc.
6535 S. Rural Road
Tempe, Arizona 85283

Printed in the United States of America

To my dear wife

iv

Contents

Introduction	vii
Chapter I, Marital Disposition	1
Chapter II, Stellar Positions in the Signs	49
Chapter III, Significant Aspects for Love and Marriage	131
Chapter IV, Celestial Bodies in the House of Marriage	141
Chapter V, The Midpoints	147
Chapter VI, Comparative Analysis Using the 90° Workboard	153
References	175

Introduction

Almost thirty-eight years have passed since the first edition of this book in German. In this interval it has become possible to obtain further substantiations of the ideas put forward in this book and to gain considerable experience, and the publication of an enlarged edition has now come about.

It is a recognized fact that certain relationships exist between the cosmos and man. The only point of dispute has been the extent to which the influence of the cosmos affects all living things. Here we must recall that the term cosmos does not apply solely to the relationship between the stellar bodies and man's character and fate but also those factors which cosmobiology has included in its realm of research, i.e. climate, geography, race, environment, etc. We are of course perfectly aware of the fact that the stars cannot "tell all"; instead man is faced with a great number of possible influences which he must confront by means of his own formative power and will in order to shape his own destiny.

The prime concern of this book, however, will be that of the relationships reigning between the stellar configurations and human character and rests on the premise that character and fate are determined to a certain extent by the natal configuration, but also that the individual himself has the power of decision as to how to shape his life on the basis of the dispositions and possibilities present to him.

In the case of two individuals entering into a relationship with one another, their natal charts can provide valuable information as to their respective dispositions and to what degree these will contribute to a harmonious or disharmonious working and living together. In the same way as the exchange of rings at the wedding ceremony symbolizes the union, so do also the dispositions contained in the natal configurations intermingle to form one unity, a "cosmic marriage." Numerous examples are presented here to prove how one can recognize whether such a cosmic marriage will develop well or poorly, harmoniously or disharmoniously.

The main purpose of this book is to illustrate that the individual should get to know himself and be able to obtain a correct picture of his partner's disposition and to recognize whether or not two persons are suited to one another on the basis of their physical, emotional and spiritual characteristics so that they can expect to live with one another in harmony.

Only very few individuals are capable of true self-perception, and one path leading to it is the thorough investigation of the individual cosmogram—the methods of investigation are discussed in detail in several textbooks[1]. Only if one has attained genuine perception of his own self will he be in a position to gain insight into and correctly assess that individual intended to share in his future. The general attitude, however, is that one's own feelings should be decisive in choosing a partner. And yet how often our feelings deceive us, and how often other considerations other than the question of true love play a role in the decision to get married. How often love and sex are taken one for the other, how often egotistical motives to improve one's social position and living conditions lie at the base of one's decision, how often title and position are the decisive factors. The past few decades have shown how these superficialities one day pale and finally dwindle to nothing in the face of profound political and economical conditions, and just how such eventualities serve as a touchstone for the durability of the union for life.

True and genuine love, which should be the foundation of every marriage, is the absolute feeling of belonging together, the certainty of only being perfectly complete in conjunction with the other person. But how are two individuals to form a harmonious union? Should they be similar types or should they complement each other? Certain similarities as to origins and milieu should be present, although there are cases where direct opposites in these respects have combined successfully. Ideas as to the goals in life must be held in common.

With regard to temperament and character, however, only complementation will provide a good basis for long-lasting harmony.

Character complementation means that one part has a plus with regard to certain aspects of his disposition, whereas the other part has a minus in the same area, and that the one individual is vivacious and the other more reserved, one has a great deal of energy at his disposal and the other is more passive in his will to activity, one is able to make snap decisions and the other prefers to wait and see. Here we see the old saying in action: Opposites attract. Kretschmer's research has shown that most marriages are marriages of contrast[2]. The individual appears to have the instinctive desire to find a partner who possesses what he himself does not have and which will complement his own being.

If therefore an individual represents a more extroverted type as according to Jung, and he is obliging, open and friendly in character, able to find his way in every situation, then an introverted type of individual would be his complement, in that this individual is more hesitative and reserved in character and is usually more on the defensive[3]. Curry has determined on a bioclimatic basis two fundamental types: the ambitious, energetic, goal-conscious K-type, who is sensitive to cold and loves a mild climate; and the emotional, amiable and pleasant W-type, who is sensitive to heat[4]. The G-type, or mixed type, exhibits characteristics of both of the above types at the same time. Experiments in the climate chamber have shown that almost without any exception marriages are made up of

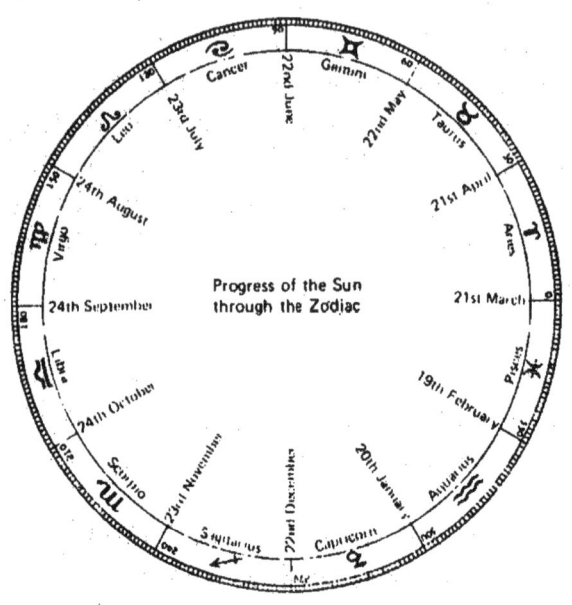

Progress of the Sun through the Zodiac

contrasting types; it was at least determinable that the one partner tended towards the W-type and the other partner towards the K-type. Whereas K- and W-types come together readily enough, the G-types are a bit slower at achieving their marital ends and generally marry a G-type.

Curry's research in particular substantiates the conviction presented in the first edition of this book that a harmonious marriage rests primarily on the complementation of character.

Popular astrology as a rule holds a completely different viewpoint, based on the solar positions in the signs of the zodiac in relation to their trine combinations.

As we know, the Sun travels through one of the twelve signs of the zodiac in one month. Someone born between March 21 and April 20, for instance, is "Aries," or someone born between April 21 and May 21 terms himself "Taurus," etc.[1]

According to a tradition thousands of years old, the signs of Aries, Leo, Sagittarius correspond to the choleric, Taurus, Virgo, Capricorn to the melancholy, Gemini, Libra. Aquarius to the sanguine, and Cancer, Scorpio, Pisces to the phlegmatic temperament[5]. Now if this folk astrology states that, for example, persons with Sun in Aries, Leo or Sagittarius, i.e. choleric types, are suited to one another, then it is every bit as wrong as to say that two phlegmatic types would be a good match. After all, two "hotheads" together could only be expected to get involved in too many arguments, whereas two phlegmatics would tend to bore one another. And where here is the lasting harmony to come from? And finally, choosing a partner for marriage cannot be done solely according to what types are supposed to suit each other, but rather a choice must be made after a careful and responsible consideration of the individual characteristics.

I
Marital Disposition

Before comparing the partners' natal charts, it is necessary first to examine the individual cosmograms separately as to their "marital disposition." Prerequisite to this is a well-founded knowledge of method and interpretation.

The first questions to be considered are those of what kind of relationship exists between the individual and his parental home, of whether there are any diseases in the family which could possibly be hereditary, or whether there are any indications to be found as to the impossibility of the marriage taking place at all. One must therefore first determine which factors in the natal chart coincide with those of the parents' charts. One finds frequently that correlations to the cosmogram of the mother or the father are especially pronounced, with the consequence that the emotional tie to one of the parents is particularly strong. If it is a case, too, of an only child, who in addition may be an introvert in Jung's definition, then ways have to be found to prevent these strong emotional ties with the parents from endangering the pending marriage. Especially difficult circumstances may arise when the partner closely attached to his family also remains living in his old home, thus being confronted with a decision between parents or partner, the makings of a first marital conflict. In one case, for example, a young woman of good family, who was very closely attached to her mother, married a young man from the same town and moved in with him in his parents' home. The young woman was unable to adjust herself to the new circumstances, and when her husband was away from home she would visit her mother daily, until she was hardly ever at home any more. The daughter's Venus was located at 25° Virgo, the mother's Venus and Sun were at 24° and 28° Virgo respectively; the daughter's Moon was trine the foregoing at 24° Capricorn. This emotional tie was so strong that it constantly overbore her relationship with her husband, and after a year she returned to her parents' home for good, and her husband filed for a divorce.

Marital difficulties are often greater when the partners concerned had a particularly happy parental home life[6].

The hereditability of any family diseases becomes all the more likely when parental configurations pertaining to illness are aligned with configurations in the cosmogram of the child. If, for instance, the mother has a kidney disorder under a strongly occupied sign of Capricorn or a negative aspect of Venus, and similar configurations are to be found in the daughter's case, then there is the great probability of the disease being passed on. The least one can do here is to see that similar configurations are not involved in the partner's case, so that the evil is not compounded. I expressly warn, however, against trying to diagnose a disease solely on the basis of the cosmogram; it is imperative to consult a physician, if possible one with astrological training. Similarly, conclusions as to procreative ability should by no means be drawn from the natal chart alone; here again, the physician's diagnosis is of primary significance. The natal chart can present certain indications, but the foundations of astro-medicine have as yet not been fully substantiated and cannot be solely relied upon.

Some people find it very easy to establish contact with others, and there are other people who feel inhibited in this respect. This "contact-ability" is generally present when the signs Gemini, Libra, and Aquarius are well occupied. When there is more accent placed on the signs Taurus, Virgo, and Capricorn, the person concerned has greater difficulty in making acquaintanceships. We find a wait-and-see attitude with Cancer, Scorpio, and Pisces, whereas a strong occupation of Aries, Leo, and Sagittarius is conducive to the desire for "conquest." Good aspects between Sun (man) and Moon (woman) are favorable for marriage prospects; unfavorable aspects between Sun and Moon can bring about a dissonance between the dreamed-of ideal and reality. Favorable configurations of Venus and Mars are indicative of a harmonious instinctual life; unfavorable aspects are apt to lead to corresponding disturbances. Good aspects between Sun and Venus conduce to a state of being in love, and often also to beauty, physical love, and strong powers of attraction.

Good Sun and Mars aspects increase vitality. Sun and Jupiter aspects make for better health. Moon and Venus aspects lead to devotedness and a strong desire for affection. Aspects between Moon and Mars are favorable to the procreative power of women in particular and motherhood, and Venus and Jupiter aspects are conducive to affection, grace, being in love, "love's bliss."

Unfavorable are critical aspects of Saturn and Neptune to Sun, Moon, Venus and Mars. Saturn unfavorably aspected to Sun and Moon fosters inhibitions; Saturn in a critical aspect to Sun brings about in a female cosmogram a disturbance in her relationship to father or husband, or to Moon affects negatively in the male cosmogram the relationship to mother or wife. Saturn in unfavorable aspects to Venus can often produce frigidity, alienation or lead to adulterous associations. Neptune unfavorably aspecting Sun and Moon frequently indicates disappointments or also illness; in aspects with Venus, peculiar or disappointing love relationships; with Mars, poor health, weakened procreative power, danger of infections.

It would be going too far afield at this point to discuss all the interpretative factors involved in the natal chart here. Those undertaking extensive investigations will in any case have to consult a comprehensive book on interpretations[7].

Within the framework of tradition, close attention is also paid to the houses in the natal chart. Emphasis is placed on the cardinal points: Ascendant (the rising point), Descendant (the declining or descending point), Medium Coeli (Midheaven, point of culmination) and Immum Coeli (celestial nadir, point directly opposite that of culmination).

The horizon divides the natal chart into two halves at the moment of birth: an upper, visible half, and a lower and invisible half. If there are many celestial bodies located above the horizon, this usually indicates those persons who find it easy to make their way in life, who are self-assertive and full of decisiveness, who are hence more active in their attitudes. With a majority of celestial bodies located below the horizon, the subconscious forces come more to the fore, and these persons are more liable to be guided by fate; at the same time, however, their inner and emotional life is richer. In this respect mutual complementation would mean the presence of a majority of bodies below the horizon in the one partner's case and a majority of bodies above in the other partner's case.

A clustering of celestial bodies at the Ascendant points to the development of a strong personality, especially when Sun, Mars or Jupiter are involved here. Saturn may be an indication of the individual's inability to develop properly and fully and of his inhibition due to environmental influences. At this position Neptune often leads to a lack of self-assertive power and to dissatisfaction or disappointment because of persons in the environment. Favorable aspects at Ascendant therefore promote a person's ability to make acquaintanceships, and unfavorable positions correspondingly lessen this ability.

The Descendant, or setting point, which is also designated as the cusp of the seventh house, supposed to be particularly applicable to marriage matters, typifies the relationship of the individual to others close to him, to the unaccustomed and different, and to the general public. Favorable bodies at this point—as long as they are not involved in unfavorable aspects—can make for a harmonious relationship to the spouse, especially when Jupiter or Venus are to be found at this spot. Saturn, Uranus, and Neptune can easily lead to inhibitions, alienation, upset, disappointment.

Favorable celestial bodies around the Immum Coeli may be indicative of a good hereditary disposition and a harmonious parental home life, whereas unfavorable bodies at this point may mean a hereditary taint or an unfortunate home life.

Favorable celestial bodies at Medium Coeli are of aid in achieving life's goals, and unfavorable bodies here can inhibit the emotional, spiritual, or vocational development.

By no means should these factors, as described above, be evaluated by themselves. They should always be considered in connection with the other configurations of the natal chart.

Having worked through the partners' charts individually, we may now proceed to relate them to one another.

Comparative Analysis

The easiest way to undertake a comparison of a married couple's stellar configurations is to lay out the two cosmograms in front of you. An ideal case is when one horoscope is the absolute reverse of the other, i.e. one has the Ascendant in Aries, for example, and the other in Libra, or the solar positions are in mutual opposition. This is the complementation referred to in the introduction. The strong-willed Aries-born needs as his complement the more adaptable Libra type, the quiet and well-adjusted Taurean counterbalances the Martian Scorpion. The lively Gemini-type is held in bounds by the more dignified Sagittarian, the consistent Capricorn type lends firmness to the pliant Cancer-born, etc. These characterizations should not be taken to be invariable, since they will be altered according to the other configurations involved.

A differentiation is made in the zodiac between positive and negative signs. The positive signs are Aries, Gemini, Leo, Libra, Sagittarius, Aquarius; the negative ones are Taurus, Cancer, Virgo, Scorpio, Capricorn, Pisces. The positive signs tend to mould the extrovert (a person adjusted to the external world), and the negative signs are formative for the introvert (a person whose thoughts and life are self-centered, inwardly directed). Hence, there is complementation when more positive signs in the one partner's case and more negative ones in the other partner's case are occupied. Again, this is not to be solely relied upon without consideration of further developments in the comparison.

We now look to see whether there are any individual heavenly bodies in the cosmograms located in the same position in the zodiac, i.e. in conjunction. Particularly favorable is the conjunction of one partner's Sun with the other's Moon, or likewise when Sun or Venus of the one is conjoined with the other's Venus, or when Jupiter of the one is conjunct the other's Sun, Moon or Venus, or when one partner's Venus is in conjunction with the other's Mars, indicating a strong sexual attraction.

The orb (radius) is generally not extended to more than 5°. This also applies to the mutual aspects, which are next in line for investigation. It is best to take one after the other, starting with the Sun in one of the cosmograms and checking to see which aspects form with the heavenly bodies, Ascendant and Midheaven in the other chart, each of the bodies is taken in this way in turn. It's a good idea while doing this to note on a sheet of paper the favorable and unfavorable mutual aspects in two respective columns. This will tell you at least numerically whether the favorable or unfavorable aspects predominate and give you a first overall view. However, not only the number, but also the potency of the individual configurations are to be taken as criteria. Significant aspects are underlined and given a higher value. Conjunctions or good aspects between Sun, Moon, Venus, Mars and Jupiter will be especially stressed. Close attention should however also be paid to conjunctions or unfavorable aspects of Saturn, Neptune, Uranus or Pluto to Sun, Moon, Venus, Mars, Jupiter.

Conjunctions can always be counted as especially strong, trines can be seen as strong and good, sextiles are weak. Squares and oppositions are strong, but cannot be said to be unfavorable in every case; it all depends on whether a benefic such as Sun, Moon, Venus, Jupiter, or a malefic such as Mars, Saturn, Uranus, Neptune, Pluto, is involved.

Those who are doing such investigations for the first time will perhaps be disappointed to find very many unfavorable configurations alongside the favorable ones. As we all know, no individual's life runs its course without some strokes of fate, and no marriage remains free of difficulties and upset.

Unfavorable configurations demand steadfastness and firmness in the face of crisis and find release in the form of illness, death, economic and financial difficulties. In this respect, then, no one should be afraid of getting married when many harmonious aspects are accompanied by some critical configurations. If there is a strong feeling of belonging together, then the ties will become all the more close through suffering and travail. It has often been the case that facing up to crises together and standing the test in times of trouble have resulted in true mutual understanding and estimation, making the bonds of marriage even stronger.

The correct assessment and interpretation of marriage cosmograms requires a great deal of experience. Only when a great number of cases have been looked into can anyone expect to attain a certain degree of sureness, and, therefore, any premature conclusions should be avoided when only a few cases have been considered.

Let us now do some practical investigations of some cases.

A Happy Marriage

Female nativity on May 31, 1889, 2:00 p.m., Augsburg, Germany.
Male nativity on December 8, 1878, 11:30 a.m., Augsburg.

In figure 2 we find the woman's natal configurations entered in the outer ring, the man's are in the middle ring, and the day of the marriage, April 5, 1910, is in the inside ring. (The number of degrees have been rounded off to make the chart easier to read.)

The solar positions of the two cosmograms are within a few de-

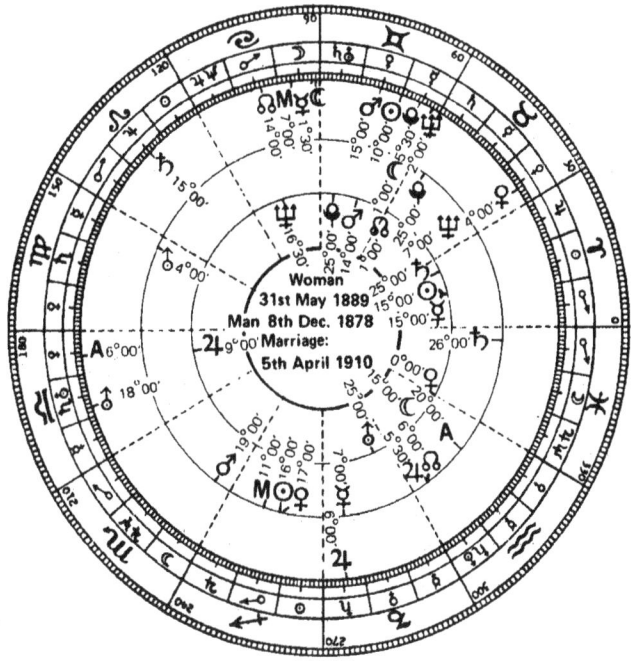

Figure 2

grees of being in exact opposition to one another in the signs Gemini and Sagittarius. Consulting one of those superficial astrological marriage books to decide the question of what man or what woman is the right mate for you, the answer one would get would be that these two individuals do not suit each other because of the solar opposition. Yet this woman's letter does give the impression that her marriage is a harmonious one. She wrote: "Our sole consolation in these times of almost unbearable worry is our beautiful and harmonious marriage together. We have never had any serious conflicts in all the years we've been together, even though we are so different in character." This very difference in character, however, means complementation. This marriage continued in harmony, the husband died in 1950, and the wife was inconsolable. The marriage did have one weak point, and that was that no children came of it. But even this disappointment did not disrupt their bond.

As regards the "marital disposition," the wife had a Jupiter-Venus trine, which generally indicates happiness (Jupiter) in love (Venus); Sun trine Ascendant, indicating a harmonious personality; Mercury conjunction Moon, pointing towards an emotional way of thinking; and Mars conjunction Sun trine Uranus reveals energy and activeness. Less favorable is the Mars position between Moon and Neptune (Mars = Moon/Neptune), which indicates a subdued instinctual life or a disorder in the female genital organs.

In the husband's case, Sun conjunction Venus points toward strong feelings of love, Jupiter conjunction Moon's Node is favorable to relationships, involving here as well a trine to Moon, making for a happy (Jupiter) relationship (Moon's Node) to the wife (Moon). A certain degree of disappointment is to be concluded from the square of Neptune to Jupiter and Moon's Node respecting the lack of children.

A compilation of all the mutual aspects gives us the following picture:

Harmonious Aspects
Sun m trine Saturn w
Venus m trine Saturn w
Venus m sextile Uranus w
Sun m sextile Uranus w
Mercury m conjunct Jupiter w
Mercury m trine Venus w
Neptune m trine Jupiter w
Jupiter m trine Ascendant w
Moon's Node m trine Ascendant w

Jupiter m trine Neptune w
Moon's Node m trine Neptune w
Ascendant m trine Uranus w
Uranus m trine Jupiter w
Uranus m trine Venus w
Uranus m sextile Mercury, Moon w

Disharmonious Aspects
Sun m opposition Mars w?
Sun m opposition Sun w?
Venus m opposition Mars w?
Neptune m conjunct Venus w
Moon m conjunct Neptune w
Jupiter m square Venus w?
Moon's Node m square Venus w
Mars m square Saturn w

This synastry makes one stellar combination particularly obvious, and that is Sun conjunction Venus m (male) in opposition to Sun conjunction Mars w (female). Accordingly, this involves not only a complementation through the solar positions, but in addition, Venus and Mars influence the sexual attraction. Mercury m and Jupiter w are at the same location, i.e. in opposition to Mercury with the wife's Moon. The wife's emotional way of thinking, Mercury and Moon in Cancer, is complemented by the husband's more sober and objective way of thinking. Mercury in Capricorn. Neptune w aspecting Moon m indicates the disappointment due to the wife's sterility, which is also stressed by Venus w conjunction Neptune m.

Numerically, the favorable configurations predominate. According to tradition, opposition and square are considered to be unfavorable aspects. The most significant configurations are in bold type. The question marks identify those configurations requiring special investigation.

The favorable Saturn aspects imbue a marriage with a certain degree of solidity and durability, and these aspects can therefore be regarded as valuable.

Concerning the disharmonious aspects it has already been pointed out that the opposition of the solar positions should be interpreted as complementation. The opposition of Venus and Mars indicates sexual attraction. In fact, the absence of any Venus-Mars aspects means a lack of sexual attraction, which is necessary for long-term contentment in a relationship between man and woman. The Neptune aspects refer to the lack of children. Mars square Saturn should be regarded as very critical, but it does not necessarily have to pertain to a separation, instead it may also, as in this case, be indicative of the joint life struggle.

In order to facilitate the evaluation of the individual aspects, special "Rules of Comparative Analysis" have been included in this book, but these are of course only intended to serve as rough guidelines and can therefore not entirely replace the individual evaluation.

On this basis, then, the individual configurations are to be interpreted as follows:

- Sun trine Saturn: solidity, steadfastness.
- Venus trine Saturn: faithfulness.
- Sun sextile Uranus: mutual stimulation, encouragement.
- Venus sextile Uranus: refined sensuality.
- Mercury conjunction Jupiter: accomplishment.
- Mercury trine Venus: thinking of one another with love.
- Neptune trine Jupiter: spiritual endeavor, idealism.
- Jupiter trine AS: adjustment.

- Moon's Node trine AS: coming and being together.
- Jupiter trine Neptune: spiritual endeavor, idealism.
- Moon's Node trine Neptune: spiritual bond, platonic love.
- AS trine Uranus: sudden experience.
- Uranus trine Jupiter: experiencing joy and happiness.
- Uranus trine Venus: affection, refined sensuality.
- Uranus sextile Mercury: the realization of joint plans.
- Uranus sextile Moon: great mutual affection.
- Sun opposition Mars: extreme exercise of will to overcome failures and crises.
- Sun opposition Sun: complementing characteristics.
- Venus opposition Mars: sexual attraction.
- Neptune conjunction Venus: disappointment in love.
- Moon conjunction Neptune: wrong ideas.
- Jupiter square Venus: tensions in love life.
- Moon's Node square Venus: disadvantageous love relationship.
- Mars square Saturn: suffering, separation.

On the whole, this synastry can be considered a good one, even if some disharmonious configurations indicate life crises.

Let us now take a look at the configurations for the day of marriage, April 5, 1910. The mundane constellation for this day was in itself favorable. Sun and Mercury conjoined in Aries and at the same were located sextile to Mars, Moon formed on this day a trine to Jupiter and Mars; however, Sun and Mercury were also approaching the square to Neptune, the disappointer.

The more striking transits on this day for the wife were:

- Sun, Mercury sextile Mars
- Sun, Mercury trine Saturn

- Moon trine Mars, Uranus
- Moon opposition Saturn
- Venus square Neptune
- Venus trine Mercury, Moon
- Moon's Node conjunction Neptune
- Mars conjunction Mars
- **Jupiter conjunction AS**
- **Jupiter trine Sun**

There are good prospects ahead in life and for a good marriage thanks to the favorable Jupiter position.

The husband has the following configurations:

- Sun, Mercury trine Sun, Venus
- **Moon's Node conjunction Moon**
- Mars opposition Sun, Venus
- Venus square Moon's Node

Jupiter retrograde approaches trine Moon's Node, Jupiter. The strongest transits are Moon's Node conjunction Moon (relationship with the wife) and the pending trine of Jupiter to Moon's Node and Jupiter.

Let us now calculate the solar arc directions according to the rough key for 1 year = 1° (this to avoid complicated calculations in our investigation), and, characteristically, the female chart has Sun and Moon 21° apart, and the age at marriage was 21. The trine to the Venus on the day of marriage is at the same also located here. Directional relationships between Sun and Moon are characteristic of partnerships[8]. Simultaneously, the progressed Sun conjoined with Mercury, which appertains to vocational success, travel, changes of scenery. Mars advanced by 21° reaches 6° Cancer, i.e. the opposition to Jupiter, forcing a decision, in this case, the decision to get married. Jupiter-Mars aspects very frequently play a role in marriages. Saturn advanced by 21° reaches the trine to Jupiter, which indicates a good relationship to older persons. The husband was ten years older than she.

Considering the progressive configurations according to the key 1 year = 1 day after birth, we find that the configurations for June 21, 1889, are of specific interest. On this date, Venus is located at 16° Taurus, thus conquering the marriage-inhibiting quadrature of Venus p to Saturn. You will very often find it to be the case that there is not necessarily a "marriage constellation" present, but that an inhibitive configuration has just been overcome.

The husband's age is already 31 years, 5 months, so that attention has to be paid to the difference of an ample 31°. Venus advanced by a generous 31° reaches a sextile to Mars: love relationship, sexual relationship. The advanced Mercury has just transited the Moon's Node, representing the thoughts of or plan for (Mercury) a relationship (Moon's Node). Uranus advanced by 31° reaches the trine to Jupiter: sudden stroke of good fortune, happy turn in life. At the same time, Uranus reaches the wife's Ascendant.

The most striking thing about the progressive aspects calculated for the 31st day after birth, i.e. January 8, 1879, is the location of Mars p at 11° Sagittarius conjunction Midheaven/Moon's Node, therefore pointing toward a turning point in life of some significance. as well as at the midpoint Midheaven/Moon's Node, pertaining to affection and sexual attraction.

Unhappily Married Twice

Female nativity on November 4, 1896, 3:00 a.m., Munich.
First husband born February 15, 1898, 3:00 p.m., 12E10, 48N30.

First marriage took place March 13, 1920.
Child born March 2, 1921, died March 10, 1921, buried March 13, 1921 (first wedding anniversary).
Divorce decreed on February 22, 1927, because of the husband's adulterous relationship with another woman, who became pregnant.
Second marriage, May 30, 1928.
Second husband born October 28, 1895, 3:00 a.m., 11E30, 48N; divorce on July 3, 1930.

This woman's natal chart shows the sign Virgo at the Ascendant square to Mars, resulting in a critical attitude towards things, easily leading to differences. Sun with Saturn and Uranus in Scorpio indicates assertiveness, pertinacity in pursuing personal goals, pronounced emotional tensions, excitable personality, and at the same time Saturn with Uranus square Moon's Node also points to poor adaptability. She lacks obligingness and affection, so that the partner will often feel rejected. The heavy occupation of the sign Scorpio may also be an indication of abdominal disorders, which can detrimentally affect the character. Mars and Neptune have Midheaven between them, making the native subject to subconscious urges; she lacks proper self-control and indulges herself too much in her moods. Moon conjunction Mercury trine Mars indicates a willpower guided by the emotions and, frequently, too much frankness and impulsiveness. The Mars element is fairly prominent in this chart, not only because of the Mars aspect to Moon and Mercury, as the most significant combination, but also because of the Sun's position in the Mars sign Scorpio. The absolutely right mate for this woman would be a man who is resilient and adaptable and who avoids any kind of conflict.

The first husband's natal chart has the sign of Leo on the Ascendant, from which we may conclude that this is a very energetic type person, who prefers always to take his fate on his own

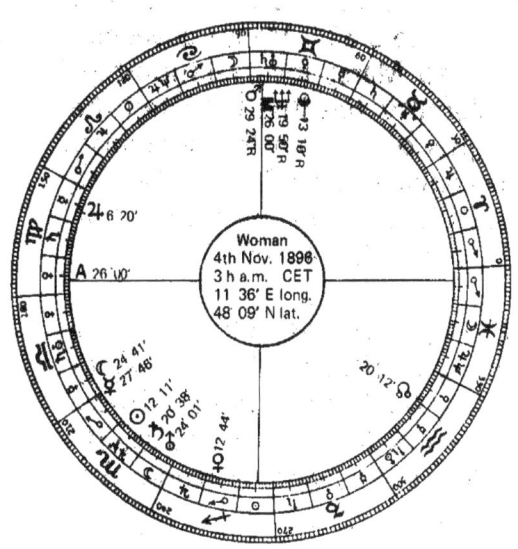

Figure 3

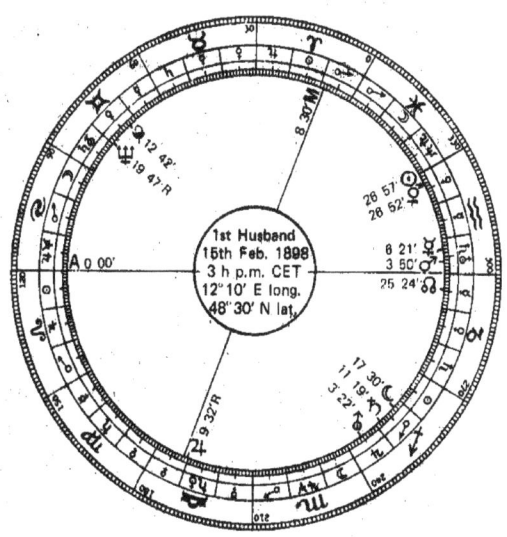

Figure 4

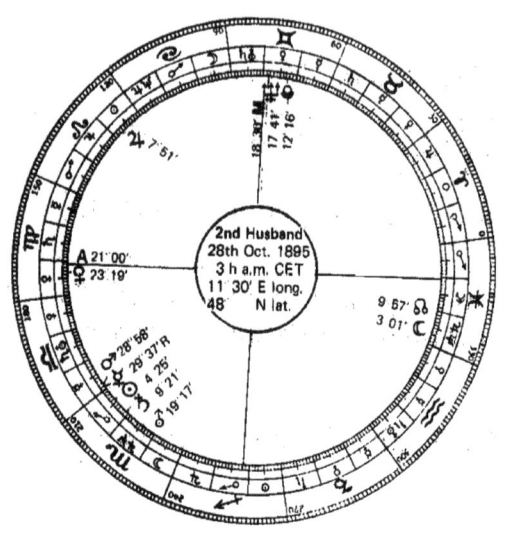

Figure 5

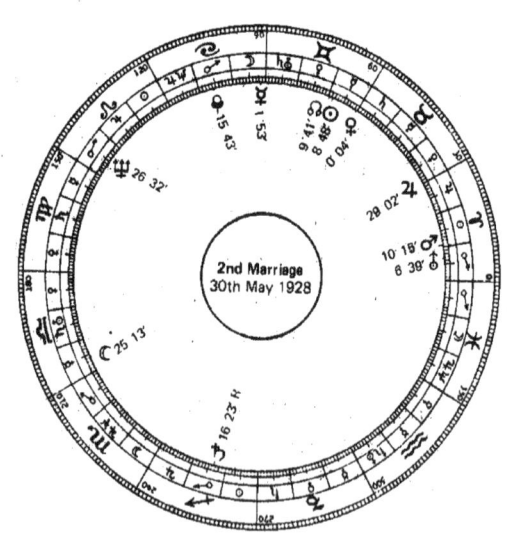

Figure 6

hands, especially so since Mars is conjunct Mercury on the Ascendant. making this individual keen on discussions and quick on the uptake. Mars and Mercury are trine Jupiter, and this man is enterprising and active and is able to assert himself in life successfully. Sun conjunction Venus in Aquarius produces in him a knowledge of human nature, knowhow in dealing with others, and makes him companionable and capable of strong feelings of love. In contrast, Moon conjunction Saturn and opposition Neptune makes him appear at times depressed and feel himself unable to develop to the full, and, due to the influence of Neptune, he is capable of deluding himself and others. The decisive development here is whether he gives in to his negative disposition or whether he consciously tries to exploit his positive characteristics. In order to determine the level of development in each corresponding case, handwriting analysis and suchlike can often be of great value.

A comparison of the two cosmograms produces the following picture:

- **Sun, Venus m trine Moon Mercury w**
- **Sun, Venus m trine Mars w**
- **Sun, Venus m square Uranus, Saturn w**
- Neptune m conjunct Neptune w
- Uranus m square Jupiter w
- **Saturn m conjunct Venus w**
- **Moon m opposition Neptune w**
- Moon's Node m square Moon w
- **Neptune m square Mars/Venus (21° Virgo)**

This summary is the reverse picture of the foregoing example. The unfavorable configurations predominate. The coincidence of favorable aspects with the unfavorable greatly impairs the effectiveness of the positive combinations. Sun/Venus m trine Moon w cannot in the long run serve to maintain a relationship

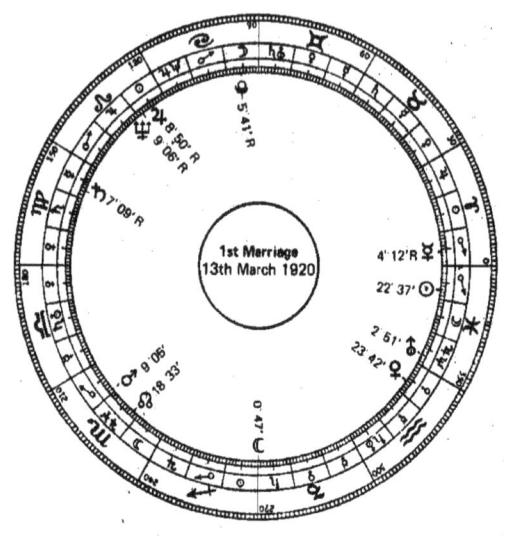

Figure 7

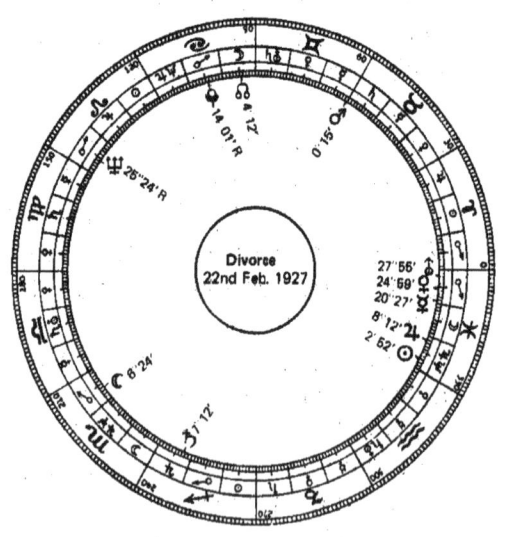

Figure 8

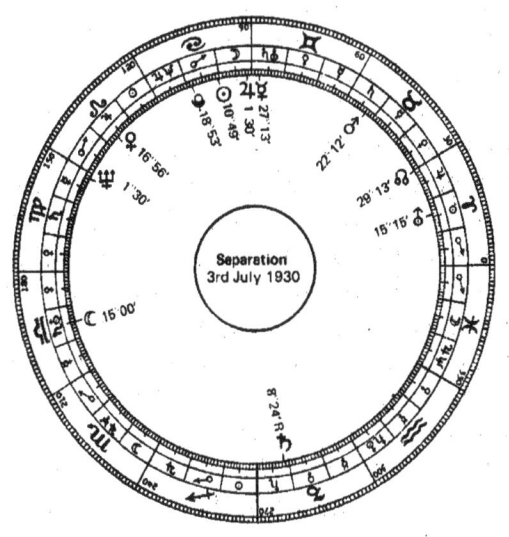

Figure 9

when at the same time this Sun is located square to Uranus w, indicating sudden or upsetting events. Venus m trine Moon w presumably allows for the development of strong feelings of love until the square to Uranus w and Saturn w leads astray and cools down the love relationship. Sun m trine Mercury w brings about personal contacts, acquaintanceships, which, however, do not necessarily have to lead to love. This aspect is therefore not very significant for love-life, although in the case of a good synastry it may increase the mutual spiritual understanding. Venus m trine Mercury w is conducive to amorous thoughts, but these may turn to the reverse under the influence of the square to Saturn w. Sun m trine Mars w promotes the joint intention of establishing a household, but Sun m square Uranus w and Saturn w detrimentally affects any joint planning.

The relationship should actually be considered a better one, if it weren't for the coincidence of good and bad aspects at points common to both cosmograms. One should always keep in mind that one day these points will be touched by transits and that the common destiny will be put on its course.

According to the rules of comparative analysis, the following indications are given by the mutual aspects:

- Sun trine Moon: spiritual harmony.
- Venus trine Moon: affection, love.
- Sun trine Mercury: personal contact.
- Venus trine Mercury: thoughts of love.
- Sun trine Mars: joint will and intention.
- Sun square Uranus: unforeseen events, upset.
- Sun square Saturn: joint care and worry, harsh destiny.
- Venus square Uranus: love aberrations, faithlessness.
- Venus square Saturn: cooling down of love.
- Neptune conjunction Neptune: joint disappointment.
- Uranus square Jupiter: sudden separation, illicit behavior.
- Saturn conjunction Venus: cooling down of love.
- Moon opposition Neptune: wrong ideas about each other, emotional confusion.
- Moon's Node square Moon: no genuine spiritual contact.
- Neptune square Mars/Venus: faithlessness, adultery.

The various indications of faithlessness were substantiated, since a divorce was granted on February 22, 1927, because of the husband's unfaithfulness. Characteristically enough, transiting Neptune was located at this time at 25° Leo in a square to Uranus of the wife and in an opposition to the husband's Sun/Venus.

Let us now make a survey of the most important directions:

There is a distance of approximately 18° between Uranus and Venus in the wife's horoscope, so that we may assume some special love experience took place at the age of 18. Approx. 30° 30' separate Sun and Venus, and hence a new love relationship came into being when she was more than 30 years old, which probably eventually led to a second marriage at the age of more than 32. At 24 years = 24° the advanced Sun reaches 6° Sagittarius, a square to Jupiter indicating the first marriage. If Jupiter is advanced by 23° = 23 years, it reaches the square to Mars around the time of the first marriage. (In the first example the resulting direction was Mars opposition Jupiter for the time of the decision to get married. Such Mars-Jupiter aspects will put in an appearance in very many marriage cases.) Advancing Venus by 24°, we find it reaches the trine to Jupiter in the 24th year of life, and the marriage was, in the beginning at least, very happy.

The husband was 22 years old at the time of the marriage, and so special attention must be paid to a distance of 22°. If Sun and Venus are advanced by 22°, they reach the square to Neptune (simultaneously also the square to the wife's Neptune), pointing toward love aberrations, disappointment or unhappy love. Mars advanced by somewhat more than 22° reaches the conjunction of Sun and Venus at the time of the marriage, indicating impulsive and premature actions and increased sensuality. We may therefore presume that the love relationship was based primarily on sexual attraction.

Conclusions as to the future course of a marriage can also be drawn from the configurations on the day of the marriage, since at the very moment when the ritual exchange of rings takes place the individual's independent life stops, from this moment on the I is bound to the Thou, the I can no longer arrange its life as it pleases. but rather must be considerate of the Thou in its life. At the beginning of cohabitation, the emanations of the two individuals comingle, they are living together, so to speak, in a joint aura. (In a comparison to the animal world, one might even speak of a joint "nest aroma." The expression, "I can't stand [the smell of] him," is more profound in its meaning than one might suppose.) The pronouncement, "I do," immediately binds the fates of two individuals, and at that moment, too, the cosmic forces play a role similar to that at the time of birth when the individual human being first sees the light of the world as a representative of his sex; in the case of marriage, this moment means the birth of the communal life, the family.

The exact time of the marriage is not known, so that the midday positions may be used here. Jupiter in conjunction with Neptune, square Mars, indicates a decision (Mars square Jupiter), leading to a disappointment (Neptune). Saturn is located exactly in the middle between Sun and Venus, a possible indication of love cooling down and a separation. This Saturn has just transited the wife's Jupiter position and in the form of a square reaches the middle of Saturn and Uranus.

Transiting Neptune is located sextile to the husband's Jupiter, and yet this aspect cannot be fully effective, since Jupiter/Neptune square Mars is due in the mundane position. The wife's natal chart has transiting Neptune almost square to Sun and Mars approaching Sun.

Transiting Venus is nearly conjunct Venus m and square Uranus w. The fact that no good interpretation accrues to Venus in the marriage horoscope can be seen from its position in the middle between Saturn and Neptune, an indication of love suffering. (The implementation of the intersecting points or midpoints, also called half-sums, will be discussed in the concluding portion of this book.)

Genuinely good prospects are not contained in the marriage

cosmogram. Its significance is evidenced by the **configurations for the date of divorce, February 22, 1927**. Transiting Sun at 2° 52' Pisces forms an exact conjunction with Uranus of the day of marriage and brings a release of the tension indicated by Saturn opposition Uranus. Transiting Moon at 6° Scorpio (noon) triggers here the square of Mars to Neptune with Jupiter. Neptune t has transited the opposition to Venus, although one should bear in mind that the disappointment (Neptune) in love (Venus) most likely took place before this. Transiting Uranus is located here at 27°55' Pisces, nearly in the middle between Sun and Mercury of the marriage horoscope, and according to CSI[7] this indicates a change in life, i.e. in this case a change from the state of being married to that of being single again. Saturn t at 7° 12' Sagittarius here reached a square, exact almost down to the minute, to Saturn of the wedding day. This configuration is in any case present again in seven years, because it takes Saturn around seven years to travel through one-fourth of the zodiac. And according to popular belief every marriage goes through a so-called seventh-year crisis. That is to say, if a marriage has lasted seven years, the chances are good for it to continue to do so; of course, there are always exceptions. We now recall that Saturn in the marriage cosmogram in the middle of Sun/Venus indicated a separation in love, which is now triggered by transiting Saturn. A few days previously, Jupiter t at 8° 12' Pisces crossed the opposition to Saturn of the wedding day. In the wife's case, the transit Saturn conjunction Jupiter was due on the wedding day, on the day of the divorce. Jupiter square Saturn was in the firmament. Looking at these cohesive factors, one must admit that these are not coincidental or arbitrary, but rather the cosmograms of the marital partners, of the day of marriage and of divorce are all consistently interrelated.

Equally of interest are the **progressive aspects** at the time of marriage and of separation. Taking the key 1 day = 1 year and applying it to the wife's case, we find the wedding day at the age of more than 23 years of life corresponds to 23 days after birth, i.e., November 27, 1896, and the day of divorce at the age of some 30 years results in December 4, 1896, the 30th day after birth.

In accordance with the year of the marriage, the following constellations were due on November 27, 1896:

- Sun p 5° 47' Sagittarius square Jupiter: success in life. (The square of the two "benefics" Jupiter and Sun need not necessarily be considered as unfavorable.)
- Saturn p 23° 25' Scorpio approaches the conjunction to Uranus, which in a few years will be exact and therefore points to a future separation.
- Mars p 24° 53' Gemini is retrograde and approaches the trine to Moon, indicating marriage and motherhood. Venus p 11°25' Capricorn approaches the sextile to Sun, to be interpreted as relative to a love relationship, marriage, conception, when other configurations also provide similar indications. (The sextile as direction should be considered more potent than a transit.) The progressive aspects presage on the one hand the possibility of marriage and on the other the future separation.

Due according to the **year of divorce** on December 4, 1896:

- Sun p 12° 53' Sagittarius has just crossed the Venus position. Whether or not at this time a new love relationship has started cannot be determined.
- Saturn p 24° 13' Scorpio has just left the Uranus position, so that here the separation configuration became due which was already pending at the time of the marriage.

In **the husband's case**, the year of the marriage finds its correspondence in March 9, 1898, and March 16, 1898 is in accordance with the year of the divorce. The following fell due the **year of the marriage:**

- Sun p 19° Pisces square Neptune, indicating disappointment.
- Jupiter p 7° 27' Libra retrograde is nearly trine Mercury, which however only falls due nine years later, when the divorce will already have become final. Special attention should be paid to the careful calculation of the progressive aspects, especially in the case of the slowmoving bodies, which often move progressively only a few minutes of one day or of one progressive year.
- Venus p 24° 16' Pisces (25°31' the following day) in sextile to Moon's Node typifies a love relationship.
- Mars p at 20°52' Aquarius reaches the conjunction with Sun, Venus only after the divorce.

The progressive aspects indicative of a marriage can only be regarded as very weak in this case.

Due at the time of the divorce:

- Jupiter p 6° 36' Libra retrograde approaches the trine to Mercury, so that this was probably happier in the subsequent years.
- Mars p 26° 19' Aquarius in an approximate conjunction with Sun, Venus relates to the second love relationship.
- Venus p 3° Aries trine to Uranus is also relative to the new love relationship.

In this light one may assume that the divorce was less painful for the man than for the woman.

The **second husband's natal chart,** October 28, 1895, 3:00 a.m., has on the Ascendant the sign Virgo as in the wife's case, so that in this respect this involves a disposition of similarities and not of complementation. All considerations are made from the personal standpoint and for egocentric motives, whereas there is difficulty in the identification with others and in adapting to others. Sun in Scorpio in conjunction with Saturn—again similar to the wife's case—is to be considered unfavorable. The separation to come already has its roots in this configuration. Sun and Saturn square to Jupiter point out marital difficulties and, at times, impediment of marriage. He was more than 32 at the time of marriage. Sun trine Moon can be seen to favor life together, but this trine cannot fully assuage the Saturn influence. Mars in conjunction with Mercury in Libra corresponds to the Mercury-Mars conjunction in Aquarius in the first husband's case. Obstinacy and quarrelsomeness endanger any getting along and living together with others, whereby the influence of the sign Libra does allay this somewhat. Love-life is guided too much by intellect due to Venus in Virgo. Saturn is located here between Uranus and Mars, Mercury, which often leads to strong inner tensions, frequently the cause of upsets involving others. Typical here is the positioning of Mercury and Mars in the middle, i.e., at the midpoint of Neptune and Moon's Node, which according to CSI[7] signifies: having the wrong ideas about relationships, inability to adapt, disharmonious living together. The woman stated in her account that this man was very egotistical and quarrelsome. This is clearly demonstrated by the following incident: On May 30, 1930, the woman was called to her father's deathbed and remained in her parents' home until he died on June 4, 1930. Although his mother took care of the household during the wife's absence, he severely berated her on her return for having stayed away so long and threatened to stab her.

This was followed up by the divorce on July 3, 1930.

The synastry of the cosmograms showed the following result:

- Moon m trine Sun w (9° orb?): spiritual harmony.
- Moon's Node m trine Sun w: harmonious union.
- Jupiter m trine Venus w (7° orb?): happy love relationship.
- Venus m sextile Saturn w: faithful union.
- Venus m sextile Uranus w: short-lived attraction.
- Mars m trine Mars w: joint success.
- Mercury m trine Mars w: joint accomplishment.
- **Venus m conjunction AS w: physical attraction.**
- Neptune m trine Moon's Node w: spiritual ties.
- Ascendant m conjunction Ascendant w: similarities of disposition and interests.
- Sun m conjunction Sun w: similar dispositions.
- **MC m conjunction Neptune w: disappointment.**
- **Saturn m conjunction Sun w: inhibitions, difficulties, danger of separation.**
- **Uranus m conjunction Saturn w: violent separation, separation through tragic fate.**
- **Uranus m conjunction Uranus w: joint upsets.**
- Uranus m square Moon's Node w: alienation, incidents.
- Moon m opposition Jupiter w: vacillating between one's fancy and a legitimate union.
- Moon's Node m opposition Jupiter w: disharmonious relationship.
- Moon's Node m square Venus w: disadvantageous love relationship.
- **Neptune m conjunction Neptune** w: joint disappointment.
- Jupiter m square Sun w: differences of opinion.
- Venus m square Neptune w: confusion, unfaithful ness, disappointment.

- Venus m square Mars w: sensual tumult and subsequent coming down to earth.
- Venus square Mars/Neptune w: wrong ideas about love.

The only favorable aspect in this synastry which can be regarded as strong is Venus conjunction AS, due to which the two partners came together in the first place. Not only do the unfavorable aspects predominate, but they are also particularly powerful. The **marriage cosmogram of May 30, 1928,** has firstly Sun in conjunction with Moon's Node, characteristic of relationships and associations. Saturn is located precisely in the middle of Venus and Mercury, so that thoughts of love (Mercury/Venus) can be easily transformed into thoughts of separation (Saturn). At the same time Saturn is at the midpoint of Uranus/Neptune, possibly signifying instability, pessimism, and separation. Venus at the midpoint Mercury/Jupiter is a configuration of the state of falling in love and of being enraptured.

Comparing the marriage cosmogram with the husband's natal chart, we find that Sun and Moon's Node are sextile Jupiter, tending to further a relationship. Mercury t has just crossed the trine to Mars and Mercury and is approaching the trine to Moon, indicating the decision to get married. In addition, on the afternoon of the wedding celebration. Moon t enters a conjunction with Mars and Mercury. Saturn retrograde has just transited the opposition to Neptune, and this same aspect recurs a few months later and is certainly evocative of the first great disappointment or falling-out, Uranus t approaches the trine to Jupiter, making the marriage appear at first sight to be a happy turning in life. Jupiter at 29° Aries opposes Mars with Mercury, a characteristic configuration for a vital decision. Such Mars-Jupiter aspects have been determined many times over in previous examples. In summary, there are certainly marriage combinations present, however, the disadvantageous aspects are not wanting either.

The wife has Moon transiting the radical Moon with Mercury and trine Mars, a similar position to that of the husband. Saturn retrograde has transited the opposition to Neptune and is approaching the conjunction with Venus, its own actual position is square to the middle of Venus/Neptune, indicating disappointed feelings of love. Mars in an approximate trine to Venus heightens sexuality. Jupiter is promotive in the sextile to Mars. Venus at 0° Gemini enters the axis Venus/Saturn the following day, probably the first occasion of a disillusionment.

The marital directions in the husband's case are roughly determined for an age of 32½ by distances of approximately 32°. Accordingly, the advanced Sun reaches the trine to Jupiter, which can be considered to be a fortuitous marriage direction. Jupiter advanced enters an opposition to the Ascending Node. i.e. a conjunction with the Descending Node, in no way good for a relationship.

The progressive celestial bodies are computed for the 32nd day after birth, i.e., for November 29, 1895. Sun at 7° Sagittarius is trine to Jupiter, since the advanced and progressive positions have to coincide in the Sun's case. Jupiter p 9° 08' Leo is approximately square to Saturn, pointing to marital (Jupiter) difficulties (Saturn), even though this aspect is not exact (a 16' difference). Good Venus-Mars aspects are completely missing. At her second marriage the woman was also nearly 32 years old. Unfortunately, the advanced Sun has already transited Venus, it is nevertheless possible that this configuration was previously instrumental in bringing about their acquaintanceship.

December 6, 1896, is the basis of calculation of the woman's progressive configurations. Only Mercury at 19° 13' Sagittarius in opposition to Neptune is due here, and this is indicative of a great disappointment.

The day of separation, July 3, 1930 has Neptune at 1°30' Virgo, in an approximate opposition to Uranus in the cosmogram of the first marriage, indicating confused circumstances. Although the man leaves the home, no divorce is decreed for lack of substantial grounds, since the wife cannot be given any blame for her visit to her father's deathbed. Jupiter 1°30' Cancer approaches the trine to Uranus, so that the solution might be called satisfactory.

The wife has the following transits due: Saturn retrograde at 8°24' Capricorn approaches the trine to Jupiter, which can be designated as a happy (Jupiter) separation (Saturn). Jupiter at 1°30' Cancer has just transited Mars, and again a decision has been made. Mars at 22° 12' Taurus is in exact opposition to the midpoint Saturn/Uranus, which according to the CSI means the "violent release of tension." Mercury at 27° 13' Gemini has transited the trine to Moon and is now located exactly trine to Mercury and approximately conjunct MC/Mars, bringing an end to the marital conflict (Mercury/Mars).

The following transits are involved on the husband's side: Sun at 10° 49' Cancer has just transited the trine to Saturn and Moon's Node, i.e. the Sun is located simultaneously at the midpoint of Saturn/Moon's Node, and the interpretation of this according to the CSI is: "The desire for seclusion, the tendency to feel uncomfortable or hindered in the presence of others. The separated husband . . ." This interpretation couldn't be any more apt. Neptune at 1°30' Virgo is approaching the opposition to Moon, to be interpreted as meaning disappointment (Neptune) due to a woman (Moon). In contrast, Jupiter at 1°30' Cancer in a trine to Moon can be considered to mean a feeling (Moon) of happiness (Jupiter) or a happy (Jupiter) woman (Moon). Mercury 27° 13' Gemini enters the trine to Mars and Mercury on the following day, so that a similar configuration to that in the wife's case forms here as well.

This concludes for the time being our outline of the investigation of the marital disposition in the individual natal charts, the comparison or synastry of the partners' cosmograms, the calculation of the transits and directions for the day of marriage.

Rules of Comparative Analysis

As far as I know, no clear and comprehepsive introduction to the systematic investigation of partner cosmograms employing specific rules of comparative analysis had been published up until the first edition of this book. These rules are to be understood only as a derivation from the usual interpretative formulas. The abbreviated form of the combinations, however, do much towards making the work easier and lending sureness. Yet no rule is without its exception, every rule is merely a tool, decisive are the random combinations of the interpretative elements. This should definitely be borne in mind, even in cases where the combinations given here hit the mark with astonishing accuracy, as has been often attested to by the many readers of the earlier editions of the book at hand.

The individual statements are not bound to any particular work method, but rather they represent a synthesis of tradition and recent research; they are not based solely on the nature of the aspects, but rather primarily on the combination of the natures of the individual stellar bodies. It is up to the observer whether a configuration of interpretative factors should be regarded as favorable or unfavorable, since only the sum of the various aspects involving a particular heavenly body may be decisive—what is called its "cosmic state"—and not the individual aspect for itself. For instance, if the Sun forms a trine to Venus and, at the same time, a square to Saturn, the trine will by no means become fully effective in a favorable sense, however, the unfavorable effect of the square will be alleviated to some degree; there is also the added possibility that transits or directions at one time will allow for the favorable influence and at another the unfavorable influence to become manifest.

Frequently in comparative analysis the individual stellar configurations are attributed with a meaning different from that accruing to them in the interpretation of an individual natal chart. Sun conjunction Sun may designate a similarity of disposition, which is not as favorable as a dissimilar or complementary disposition, as expressed in the synastry, so that an opposition can be regarded as favorable in that it indicates complementation of character. If, for example, a conjunction or opposition is triggered by transiting or directional bodies, a common fate is the result, the character of which is indicated by the nature of the heavenly bodies. If transiting Saturn crosses the mutual conjunction or opposition, this means remaining steadfast in a crisis, and if Jupiter transits these—even in opposition—a favorable outcome may be expected. There are enough instances known of where Jupiter in opposition to the solar position specified a genuinely favorable interpretation, as long as this was not at the same time subject to unfavorable aspects. It would be much more correct not to speak of favorable and unfavorable effects, but rather of harmonious or disharmonious aspects, of configurations which lead to attraction or to indifference or bring about a bond or a separation. However, this kind of differentiation would tend to make an overall view more difficult, and therefore, for the sake of simplicity, the individual stellar configurations have been marked either + or -. Since the conjunction enjoys particular significance in every case, it has been specially marked C. The symbols + and - generally appertain to sextile and trine, and square and opposition respectively.

When individual heavenly bodies in the partner cosmograms are located at the same point in the zodiac (e.g. Jupiter in Pisces in both cases), a corresponding similarity of disposition is the result; if the same bodies are positioned in a square or opposition, this means the presence of a complementary disposition (e.g. Mercury in Cancer and Capricorn), two bodies placed in a trine (e.g. Venus in Aries and Leo) indicate that the disposition has characteristics typical of the nature of the body involved.

Sun : Sun
1. +C Similarity of disposition.
2. - Complementary characteristics.

Sun : Moon
3. +C Spiritual harmony, the blending of mind and soul, the entrance of I into Thou. (Especially favorable with Sun in the male and Moon in the female sign.)
4. - Spiritual and emotional conflicts, contradiction of mind and soul, living more alongside of than within each other.

Sun : Mercury
5. +C Thinking of one another, personal contact, mental and spiritual stimulation.
6. - Disturbance of the connection through thought. (When other critical configurations are also involved.)

Sun : Venus
7. +C Strong mutual attraction, strong tie, harmonious sex life.
8. - Disharmonious sexual relationship. (Opposition and square may only be evaluated as unfavorable when other unfavorable factors are also involved.)

Sun : Mars
9. + Harmonious relationship between spirit and will, joint accomplishment, joint success.

10.   -C   Spirit and will are in contradiction to one another, conflicts and failures can only be overcome through the strictest self-control.

Sun : Jupiter
11.   +C   Joint happiness, experiencing good times.
12.   -   Differences of opinion, illicit relationship, conflicts.

Sun : Saturn
13.   +   Feeling of duty towards one another, steadfastness, stability, standing up for each other.
14.   -C   Saturn keeps the Sun from freely developing its influence, spiritual suppression of the one partner by the other, joint worries and cares, difficulties due to relations, lack of adaptability, separation.

Sun : Uranus
15.   +   Spiritual fructification, mutual stimulation, promotion and support.
16.   -C   Unforeseen incidents, mutual upset, upset and excitement due to others.

Sun : Neptune
17.   +   Spiritual relationship with high ideals.
18.   -C   Disturbed harmony due to hypersensitivity, infirmity, illness of one of the partners, disappointment, confusion and error.

Sun : Pluto
19.   +   Energetic pursual of joint aims.
20.   -C   One partner tries to suppress the other, separation, often through force majeure.

Sun : Moon's Node
21. +C Spiritual or physical relationship, harmonious living together.
22. - Disturbance of the relationship.

Sun : Ascendant
23. +C Harmonious relationship, physical suitability.
24. - Little suitability or adaptability.

Sun : MC
25. +C Joint aims in life, a relationship combining body and soul.
26. - Different goals.

Moon : Moon
27. +C Similar emotional dispositions.
28. - Dissimilar, perhaps complementary emotional dispositions.

Moon : Mercury
29. +C Thinking of one another emotionally.
30. - Doubt, interrupted contact.

Moon : Venus
31. +C Affection and love, desire for children.
32. - Strained or misguided sex life leads to disharmony, conflicts in love.

Moon : Mars
33. + Deep passion, mutual desires according to the emotions, desire for children.
34. -C Sexual relationship with pronounced tensions.

Moon : Jupiter
35. +C Feelings of happiness towards one another.
36. - Fluctuation between one's fancy and a legitimate relationship.

Moon : Saturn
37. + Feeling for one another is durable and steady.
38. -C Mutual impediment and repression (Saturn pressures the other's Moon). Coming down to earth.

Moon : Uranus
39. + Sudden, strong feelings for one another, sudden mutual influence and stimulation.
40. -C Display of emotions, upset, one partner often provokes the other without any concrete reason.

Moon : Neptune
41. + Sensitive relationship, hopes founded on spirit and emotion, having great expectations of one another, being enamored.
42. -C Being deluded by feelings for another, wrong ideas about each other, error, disappointment.

Moon : Pluto
43. + Strong emotional relationship.
44. -C Emotional shock.

Moon : Moon's Node
45. +C Spiritual relationship.
46.   Disrupted spiritual contact.

Moon : Ascendant
47. +C Spiritual-physical attraction, reciprocal influence.
48. - Attraction with subsequent disharmony.

Moon : MC
49. +C Spiritual immersion in one another, strong spiritual bond.
50. - Spiritual suffering, disruption of spiritual contact.

Mercury : Venus

51. +C Thinking of one another with love, being allied through thoughts of love.
52. - Amatory thoughts going astray, taking love too easily.

Mercury : Mars

53. + Joint aims, cooperation, joint accomplishments.
54. -C Reciprocal irritation and provocation, upsetting, harras-ment, conflict due to the nervous-irritability of one of the partners.

Mercury : Jupiter

55. +C Thoughts of mutual happiness and activity resulting in success and accomplishment.
56. - Dishonesty towards each other, conflicts.

Mercury : Saturn

57. + Serious exchange of ideas, desire to solve difficult problems.
58. -C Thoughts of separation, being frequently apart (because of vocation, travel, etc.).

Mercury : Uranus

59. + Reciprocal stimulation, realization of joint plans.
60. -C Reciprocal upset and provocation, desire to alter the other's way of thinking.

Mercury : Neptune

61. + Acceptance of the thoughts of the other, mutual thought transference.
62. -C Indulging in wrong ideas about the other, self-delusion.

Mercury : Pluto
63. + Mutually influencing ways of thinking.
64. -C Contradictions, opposite opinions.

Mercury : Moon's Node
65. +C United in thought.
66. - Going astray in thought.

Mercury : Ascendant
67. +C Good entertainment, pleasant times together, social ties.
68. - Little reciprocal stimulation, false judgement of each other.

Mercury : MC
69. +C Mutual understanding, meaning much to each other, joint delving into problems.
70. - Contradictory ways of thinking.

Venus : Mars
71. + Harmonious physical adjustment, happy satisfaction, ever-new mutual fascination, show of sexual inclinations.
72. -C Love at first sight, sensual rapture followed by sudden coming down to earth, excess desire leads to disadvantages, alienation, illness.

Venus : Jupiter
73. +C Happy love relationship, lover's bliss.
74. - Discrepancies in matters of decency and morals, love without the legal bonds of marriage, tensions in love-life. (Opposition is not necessarily unfavorable.)

Venus : Saturn
75. + Faithfully united. Marriage for practical reasons.

76. -C Cooling down of love, coming down to earth, separated love. (Love for sale?)

Venus : Uranus
77. + Love at first sight, attraction and love of short duration.
78. -C Amorous escapade, aberrations in love, unfaithfulness.

Venus : Neptune
79. + Platonic love, mutual "adoration," rare kind of spiritual love.
80. -C Disappointment, going astray, perversity, unfaithfulness. (Infection.) Yearning for love and finding no fulfillment, jealousy.

Venus : Pluto
81. + Being madly in love with the partner, feeling drawn to a love partner as if under some inner compulsion.
82. -C Voluptuousness, immorality, excesses lead to alienation.

Venus : Moon's Node
83. +C United in love.
84. - Disadvantageous love relationship.

Venus : Ascendant
85. +C Acquaintanceship turning to love, physical attraction.
86. - Disharmonious sexual relationship. (Opposition is not unfavorable.)

Venus : MC
87. +C Individual love, spiritual tie, sincere affection.
88. - Spiritual conflicts. (Opposition not unfavorable.)

Mars : Jupiter
89. +   Making felicitous agreements, becoming engaged, marrying.
90. -   Being confronted with momentous decisions, philosophical. religious or legal conflicts.

Mars : Saturn
91. +   Overcoming joint suffering, survival in crisis.
92. -C Harsh fate, becoming separated.

Mars : Uranus
93. +   Sudden, shared experience, dangers overcome.
94. -C Rebelling against each other, severe upsets, violence.

Mars : Neptune
95. +   Dependency on the will of the other, many plans.
96. -C Disunity as to intentions and actions, undermining of the relationship, mutual infection.

Mars : Pluto
97. +   Great expenditure of energy to achieve joint aims.
98. -C Violent acts.

Mars : Moon's Node
99. +   Instinctual relationship, common desires, sexual relationship.
100. -C Lack of adaptability, dispute.

Mars : Ascendant
101. +   Mutual sexual attraction and stimulation, procreative drive.
102. -C Mutual provocation, arguments and strife, violence.

Mars : MC
103. +   Mutual spiritual influence.
104. -C Emotional upset, dispute.

Jupiter : Saturn
105. +   Durable bonds, desire to keep the marriage alive.
106. -C Impediment of marriage, marital difficulties, danger of separation.

Jupiter : Uranus
107. +   Sudden acquaintanceship, hasty marriage.
108. -C Unforeseen incidents and events, great tensions, separation due to unlawful behavior of one partner.

Jupiter : Neptune
109. +   Dreams of happiness, high marital ideals, spiritual striving.
110. -C Make-believing happiness, dispersion of hopes, undermining of legitimate relationship.

Jupiter : Pluto
111. +   Joint striving for success.
112. -C Disadvantages through extravagance, joint losses.

Jupiter : Moon's Node
113. +C Good relations, happy relationship.
114. -   Disharmonious or illegal relations.

Jupiter : Ascendant
115. +C Happy acquaintanceship, good adaptability, good understanding.
116. -   Illicit relations. (Opposition is not necessarily unfavorable.)

Jupiter : MC
117. +C Feeling of bliss and happiness, joint striving for success.
118. - Fluctuating happiness. (Opposition is not unfavorable.)

Saturn : Uranus
119. + Union subject to a possible separation later.
120. -C Lack of adaptability, sudden separation, tragic fate.

Saturn : Neptune
121. + Indulging in false expectations.
122. -C Danger of gradual estrangement, unhappy circumstances, disturbance of marital happiness because of illness.

Saturn : Pluto
123. + Desire to overcome crises.
124. -C Difficult struggle in life. inability to develop separation.

Saturn : Moon's Node
125. + Desire to maintain relationship.
126. -C Lack of adaptability, one abandons the other.

Saturn : Ascendant
127. + Relationship with an older partner, sharing of experiences, faithfulness.
128. -C Inhibitions through consideration of others, one oppresses the other.

Saturn : MC
129. + Desire to overcome difficulties together.
130. -C Suffering because of the other, one oppresses the other.

Uranus : Neptune
131. + Unusual union in which supernatural or peculiar conditions could play a role.
132. -C Obscure or peculiar conditions unsettle and disturb, confused circumstances lead to separation.

Uranus : Pluto
133. + Union requires radical readjustment to circumstances.
134. -C Excitement, upset, violence.

Uranus : Moon's Node
135. + Sudden union (usually of short duration).
136. -C Excitement, upset, incidents can lead to separation.

Uranus : Ascendant
137. + Sudden coming together, sudden experience.
138. -C Exciting and disturbing circumstances.

Uranus : MC
139. + Strong emotional and spiritual influence, readjustment due to a relationship.
140. -C Emotional and spiritual excitement and upset.

Neptune : Pluto
141. + Unusual bonds of fate.
142. -C Confused circumstances.

Neptune : Moon's Node
143. + Coming together in an unusual way, platonic love, spiritual bond.
144. -C Relationship without future prospects, undermining of the relationship.

Neptune : Ascendant
145. + Indulging in mistaken ideas about the other person.
146. -C Mutual delusion, mutual make-believe, deception and deceit.

Neptune : MC
147. + Enthusiasm and rapture color attitude towards the partner.
148. -C Faking love, play-acting, soul suffering.

Pluto : Moon's Node
149. + Strange coincidences of fate.
150. -C Tragic union, separation due to unforeseen events.

Pluto : Ascendant
151. + Unusual acquaintanceship, strange attraction.
152. -C One suffers from the other, tyrrany of the one over the other.

Pluto : MC
153. + Desire to achieve joint goals with verve and energy.
154. -C One would like to misuse the other for his own ends, severe crises in life.

Moon's Node : Ascendant
155. +C Coming together, associating socially.
156. - Living together under difficult circumstances.

Moon's Node : MC
157. +C To be joined body and soul.
158. - Disadvantageous union, lack of adaptability, lack of wholeheartedness.

Ascendant : Ascendant
159. +C Similarity of disposition, similar milieu.
160. - Opposites attract.

Ascendant : MC
161. +C Physical and spiritual harmony.
162. - Complementation of physical and spiritual dispositions.

MC : MC
163. +C Similar goals and interests.
164. - Complementation of life goals.

II

Stellar Positions in the Signs

As the foregoing practical examples have shown, separate and close examination must be made of the individual natal charts before any comparison of the partner cosmograms may be attempted, in order to uncover the trends involved in the individual destinies. The following attempt to explain and interpret in detail the positions of the individual stellar bodies is presented here with the express warning not to evaluate these interpretations separately and individually. It is impossible to draw conclusions from only one single configuration: correct interpretation and assessment is only possible under consideration of the natal chart as a whole. For this reason, the variations on a theme by the popular press such as, "What man and what woman are right for you?", are thoroughly to be rejected, since they are almost always based on the solar positions.

Statistics made over the past few years on the basis of 2,500 cases involving the solar position have shown that it is indeed of particular significance, however a reliable "marital prognosis" can be only be delineated on the basis of the interplay of the solar positions with the other factors of the natal chart.

The Sun in the Signs of the Zodiac

The Sun corresponds to the spirit incarnate, the "divine spirit" in man, the "living being" per se. This derives from the solar symbol itself, ☉, a point, the spirit living and divine, surrounded by a circle, the bodily shell. Thus the Sun represents both the spirit and the body, the clean mind in a clean body—*mens sana in corpore sano*.

At the same time, the Sun corresponds to the male principle in contrast to the Moon, which epitomizes the female principle. Therefore, a strong positioning of the Sun also intensifies the male characteristics, shows the man in all his masculinity and the woman in the process of becoming more virile. The solar position can often tell us who has the upper hand in the marriage.

The Sun in Aries intensifies the masculine characteristics to a particular degree and designates men/women of action, who energetically assert their own point of view and will, who are motivated by ambition, and are keen on leadership in all kinds of situations. These are tense extroverts who are positive and electric, and who display determination, initiative, goal-consciousness, creativity, enthusiasm, alertness, self-confidence and intrepidity; they are fresh, enterprising, independent, arbitrary, proud, but they can also be hasty, hot-tempered, arrogant, and violent. Males with Sun in Aries show themselves in full masculine array, are equal to every struggle in life, demand absolute recognition and acknowledgment and stand for no opposition.

Therefore, the only permanent relationship possible for this type would be with a woman who is submissive, who looks up to and is trusting in her husband, and who on occasion can take a harsh word of his with equanimity. Arian types will frequently ally themselves with adaptable women, as a rule considerably younger than themselves. There is latent danger for the marriage when this younger wife becomes more self-sufficient and independent as she grows older, asserting her own will and no longer content with being the subordinate partner. A marital crisis is very much possible in such circumstances. A crisis can especially be brought about by the absence of the husband over a longer period of time (e.g., a trip abroad, military duty, war service or vocational activity away from home town), making it necessary for the wife to develop a greater degree of independency.

Women with Sun in Aries are just as tenacious in pursuing their goals and can develop a fighting nature, often, however, to the detriment of their femininity. These women dislike being dependent on others, are willing to take a job on the side and do not like relying solely on the household money doled out by the husband. In such cases, more adaptability is required of the husband, the wife "dominates" in the marriage. Such a woman is certainly a suitable complement for a "feminized" man. In our day and age, it is often the case that the wife has the job, and the husband has to take care of most of the household duties.

With Arian types, the life's goal often has predominance over the marriage, so that this may be broken up if it seems to stand in the way of achieving the set goals.

A religious fanatic, who has in his natal chart Sun in opposition to Jupiter and trine to Mars, divorced his first wife, because another woman was more adaptable to his philosophy of life and showed greater interest in his ideas and goats. However, he only married this second spouse after their cohabitation had caused a public sensation.

The desire to maintain one's self-sufficiency and independence is often the reason why such natures are content to do without marriage because they are better able to achieve their goals without the conjugal shackles.

The positioning of the Sun in Aries is by no means more unfavorable than in other signs, but it does make adaptability in the partner a prerequisite.

Arian types occasionally uphold especially high ideals of love and marriage, and yet would rather renounce marriage if they are unable to find the real embodiment of their ideal woman. Their yearning for sublime love remains unfulfilled, as in the case of a woman whose natal chart showed both Sun and Venus in Aries alongside various aspects obstructing marriage.

To exemplify Sun in Aries let us take the natal chart of a man (Fig. 10), who, despite a respected position, despite wealth, despite good appearance and other positive characteristics, was unable finally to take the final step towards marriage. He was engaged once, had several affaires, yet he never married. Sun is conjoined with Mercury in Aries and, additionally, trine Mars, making him too much of a rationalist and too much inclined to criticize severely, too much caught up in his vocation and his aims, and his longing for home and family, in accordance with his ideals, was not realized. Under the influence of Venus conjunct Neptune, he probably reveled often in erotic phantasies, and his disposition was a rather peculiar one, so that he was unable to find the right kind of complement. Significant here is the location of Saturn in opposition to the Ascendant, indicating a lack of adaptability.

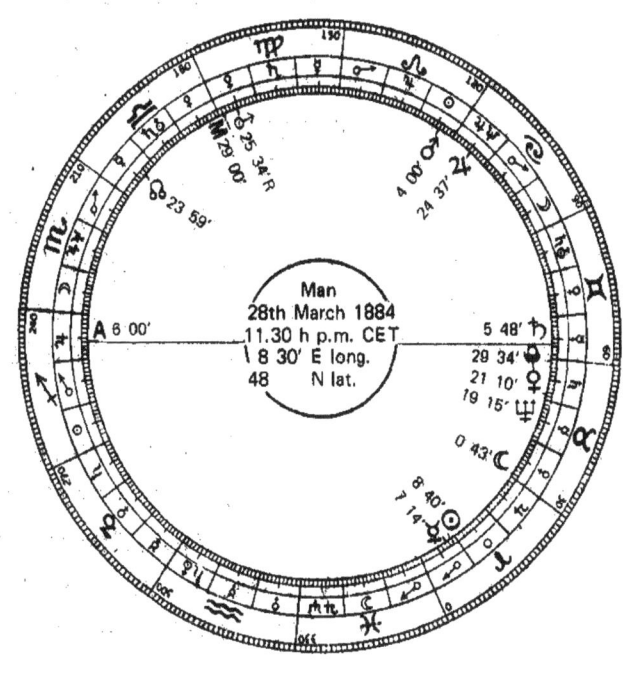

Figure 10

The Sun in Taurus makes the individual more aware of the material things in life, more interested in tangible gain and in solid foundations of life. Therefore, the question frequently asked with regard to marriage is, "What do you have, what can you offer me, is our financial basis a good one, for man cannot live from love alone!" Nevertheless, the Taureans do have within them a deep emotional life, they are kindhearted and have a great deal of sympathy, and will often do their very utmost to help others. However a certain propensity for egoism does manage to re-emerge now and again. Taureans are tense introverts, more negative and magnetic, with the aim to achieve the most carefree life possible through perseverance determination, thoroughness, presence of mind, steadfastness of principle, indefatigability, objectivity, a sense of reality, and conservatism. Passion demands early fulfillment, to the effect that often sexual desires will leave their mark on the psyche. These individuals are rarely outgoing, and then need a long time before they are able to confide in someone else; they are somewhat melancholic in nature, they tolerate rather than fight.

The men are usually good family fathers, fully conscious of their obligations, as long as there are no adverse configurations present. The Taurean women are sincere in their care of the family and are concerned with providing a harmonious and attractive home.

The Taureans enjoy any indulgence in the pleasure of life, even to the extent of extravagance, although they are capable at other times of renunciation.

It is their constant endeavor to maintain the marriage. In the case of a separation or divorce, however, they seldom remain alone, because continence means too great a sacrifice for them.

Sun in Taurus aspecting Saturn makes it very difficult to keep a marriage intact, because these individuals take everything very much to heart and are little able to overcome marital conflicts. A man with Sun in Taurus conjunction Saturn was married for nine years, was divorced, got married again, but this marriage ended in separation only six months later.

An especially tragic experience is mirrored in Fig. 11. This young girl had two lovers and was unable to decide which of them she should marry, and she therefore committed suicide. The native had a very good job in a bank, she broke of the one affair because of an illness of the man, became engaged again and then found herself in such a terrible conflict of feelings, that

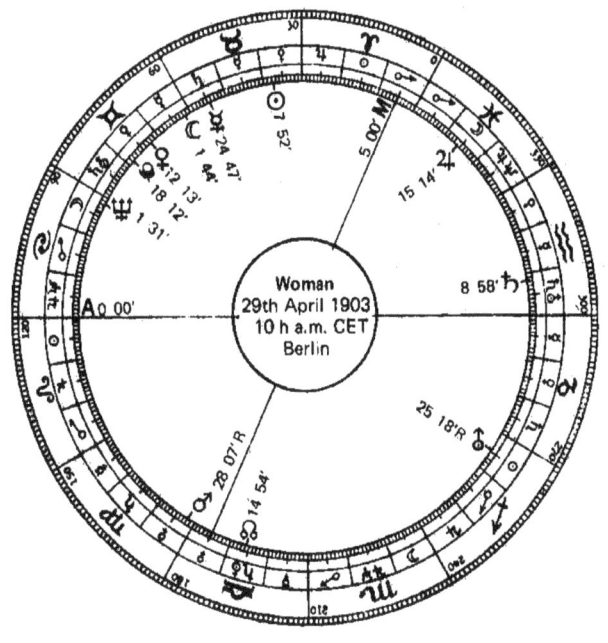

Figure 11

one evening in the absence of her parents she took sleeping pills and turned on the gas. She died August 16, 1926, just as transiting Mars was in conjunction with Sun and Moon, signifying separation (Saturn) of lovers (Sun and Moon). The decision to act derives from Uranus t opposition Mars. This example shows how emotionally tormented an individual can become through an unfavorable positioning of the Sun in Taurus, and such a person is in particular need of an understanding partner to help and stand by him. Taurus is a negative sign, and the addition of other factors signifying a negative outlook on life makes it imperative to find a marital partner with a positive and optimistic attitude towards life.

In Fig. 12, the trine of Sun in Taurus to Moon's Node is strongly uniting in character, and Moon conjunction Jupiter points to a sound emotional basis, so that the marital crises indicated by Neptune between Sun and Moon can be resolved more easily. When the wife nonetheless thought of getting a divorce, marriage counseling was yet able to prevent it. This couple stayed together and continued their life's struggle. The danger of separation was founded in the husband's frequent business trips away from home. However, the conjunction of Moon with Jupiter in the sign of Pisces predisposed to being alone frequently without too much difficulty.

Tensions are part and parcel of every marriage and are indeed necessary as a testing-ground for love and faithfulness and as a consolidation of the feeling of togetherness.

The Sun in Gemini designates the relaxed extroverts, who are positive and electric, who are active, alert, eloquent, and acute, but who may also be shallow, absent-minded and cursory. They are obliging, sociable, friendly, courteous, natural, communicative, quick, clever, energetic, but also curious, obtrusive, fickle, inconstant. Many of them are the "flighty" types, who like flitting from one flower to the other, and they are therefore in need of a partner who can give them some kind of firm hold. Both male and female types sometimes take life too lightly, they indulge in fancies and need someone who takes life more seriously.

It can be quite a good thing for an individual with Sun in Gemini to have a marital partner with both feet on the ground and who is somewhat materialistic, since the Gemini-type with his manifold interests will certainly see to it that the money finds its way into many hands as possible.

The Gemini woman wants to be able to look up to her partner, wants to dream and be enraptured, but only to be kept within

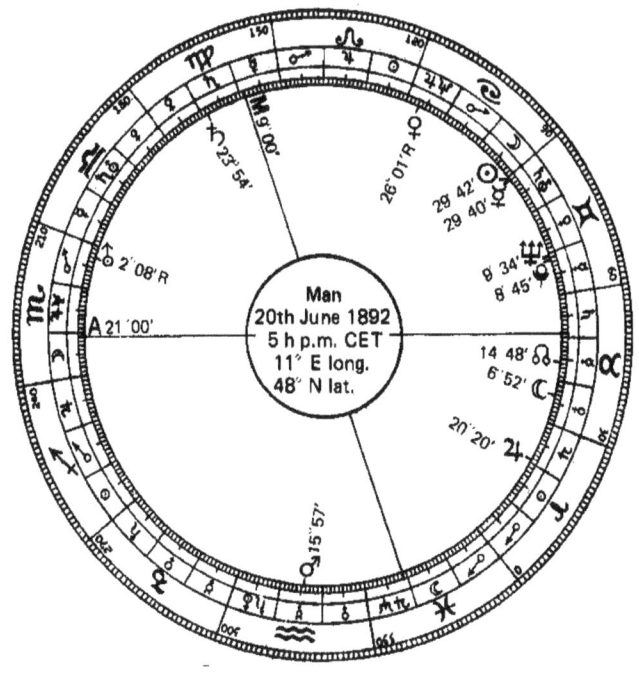

Figure 12

bounds by her partner if need be. The Gemini type will hardly endure being merely the "little woman at home" or "hubby," instead life must be stimulating and offer change, and vocational and domestic duties will be fulfilled all the more gladly.

One woman, who at birth had Sun in Gemini in opposition to Saturn, had a very difficult time of it in marriage, because the contrast between her idealistic and more generous attitude towards life and her husband's crass materialism was too great. Nevertheless the woman was able to stick by her husband up into old age, even though he was guilty of unfaithfulness and some violence. As we can see, there are some Gemini woman capable of great sacrifice.

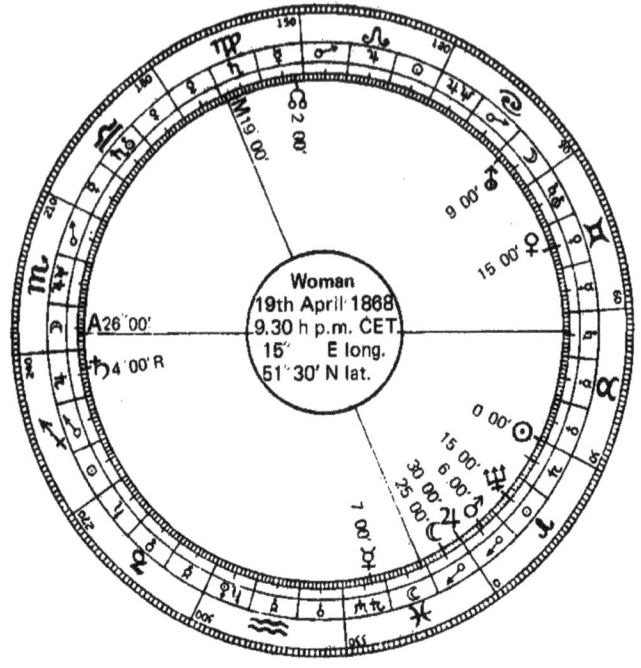

Figure 13

Fig. 13 is the natal chart of a businessman who lived very happily with his wife. However the marriage was overshadowed by the fact that children came very late in the marriage, after the wife had undergone an operation making it possible for her to have children. Hence the unfavorable opposition of Moon (woman) in Taurus to Uranus in Scorpio (procreative organs) was in this case surmountable due to the operation, and the basis for a marital conflict was eliminated. The woman was interested in the cosmic combinations and effects, and the operation was carried out successfully at a cosmobiologically favorable date.

Marital failures involving partners with Sun in Gemini are often the result of the precipitancy with which they got married in the first place and of there being no true complementation, but rather two similar types were joined together, and of the fact that Gemini types tend to take life too lightly and do not show their partners the proper kind of respect and esteem.

Sun in Cancer is usually formative of types who have at their disposal a particularly rich emotional life (lunar sign). They are magnetic and polarized negatively, belong to the relaxed introverts. who are receptive and open, impressionable, imaginative, good observers, capable of strong love, have feeling and a good sense of humor, they are amicable, affectionate, ready to help. considerate, complacent, susceptible, but also indifferent, skeptical, moody, easily embarrassed and inhibited. It is just this combination of good will and kindheartedness which makes these individuals so amiable; their modest and domestic disposition can do much towards making the marriage strong and secure. They tend to get married at a rather early age and for love, coupled with the genuine desire to become a father or mother. Hypersensitivity can on occasion lead to disharmony. The men love home and family above all and are happy when they can devote themselves to wife and children when they come home from work. The women are characterized by genuine sincerity and motherliness.

Despite their great adaptability and complaisance, their will is not to be underrated; they achieve their aims anyway—be it in a roundabout way at times. They will also do everything to keep home and marriage intact. If their love is not equally reciprocated, they will suffer greatly and make many sacrifices before they can finally decide to separate.

In the case of some individuals with Sun in Cancer, shyness and inhibition are so pronounced that they are unable to find the right mate in spite of a great longing for love.

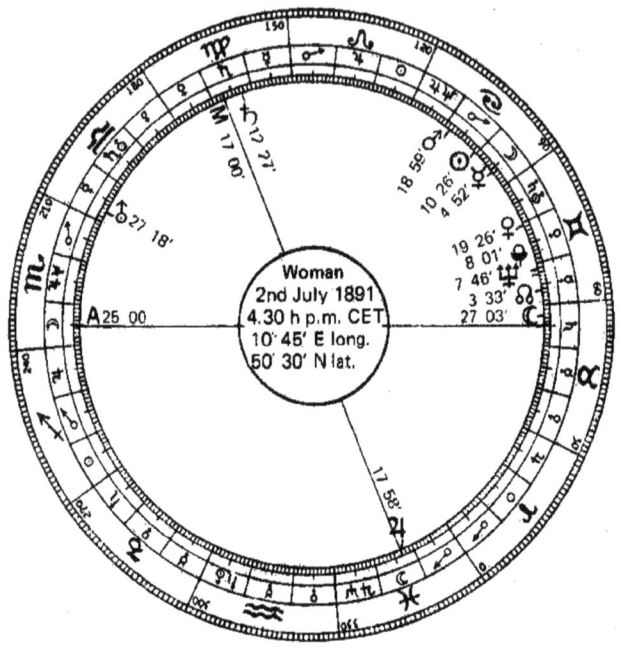

Figure 14

A lady teacher whose cosmogram had Sun in Cancer in conjunction with Saturn square Mars was condemned to a single life.

Fig. 14 is the natal chart of a woman who was very domestic and industrious. She lived with her husband for many years in completely secure and serene circumstances. But inexplicable events caused her husband to incur bad debts, he lost his job and behaved in such a peculiar way that he could be suspected of some extramarital affair. Nevertheless, this woman's love was so strong that she would not agree to a divorce despite the many difficulties and grounds present for a divorce. Disappointment and coming down to earth are represented in Venus with Neptune in a square to Saturn, whereby the square of Saturn comes between Venus and Neptune, which according to the CSI[7] means: "Tormenting oneself because of love . . . coming down to earth and becoming sober again." The marital difficulties began as transiting Neptune reached the square to the radical Neptune and the conjunction with Saturn, thus triggering the most unfavorable configuration in the natal chart. However Sun with Mars in a trine to Jupiter gave her the energy to keep up the marriage and take up the struggle to regain safe and stable conditions.

Another woman with Sun in Cancer conjunction Mars trine Jupiter and Moon was very hard put to sustain the family because of the husband's joblessness, but she managed with success. Nevertheless she was true in heart to a childhood boyfriend—without her husband's knowledge—until his death. For individuals with Sun in Cancer find it hard to forget, they retain all impressions in their hearts, even if they do not talk about them.

The Sun in Leo stands for the positive and electrically charged tense extrovert, whose main characteristics are vigorousness, initiative, goal-consciousness, determination, enthusiasm, organizational ability, sense of reality, self-assurance, exuberance, self-respect, desire for independence, undauntedness and intelligence. These individuals are eager, enterprising, circumspect, trustworthy, superior, class-conscious, proud, distinguished, generous, sociable, companionable, but also frequently careless, arrogant, presumptuous, contradictory, boastful and conceited. Getting married is not always for reasons of love, but often out of convenience, for love of wealth, title, splendor and honours, in order to increase their self-importance. The men often act like "lords of creation," then want to cut a fine figure, want to lead and give the tune, and demand subordination. The women often spend too much on clothes and

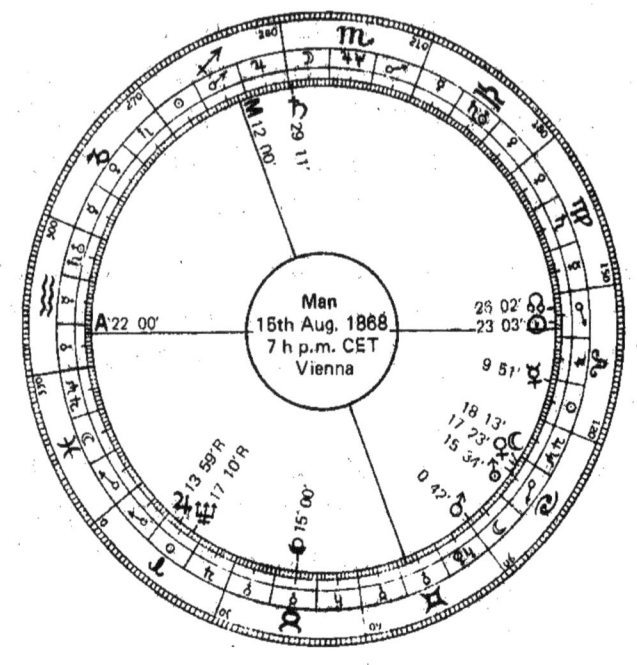

Figure 15

luxury, so that their husband's wallet doesn't always contain enough to satisfy all their desires, while they want the presence of servants to do all the work so that nothing will smudge their fingers.

The Leo type maintains his good-naturedness only so long as he is doing all right himself. Bad times and modest circumstances will see them unsatisfied, in debt, or trying to live off others. However, you will find among Leo types outstanding individuals, who are equal to any situation and who will exert all their energy to overcome a crisis, and who are faithful and devoted husbands or wives. It all depends on the relationship between Sun and the other stellar bodies.

Fig. 15 represents a very unusual case. This is a Viennese writer, who was illegitimately born of wealthy parents, who due to a stock market failure lost everything. At the age of 24 years, the native had to undergo an operation because of a venereal disease as result of an extended sex-life. Neptune square to Venus, Uranus and Moon in the radix is an indication of this. One year later he married a girl of poor family, which actually does not correspond to the Sun's position in the sign Leo. He describes the union as a marriage for love. Great difficulties arose because of his father (Sun square Saturn), who considered the marriage to be a mesalliance. The father even went so far as to curse his son on the day of the wedding. The wife died four years later. He only remarried when he was already forty years old, but this marriage turned out to be a disappointment. Later, the native indulged more and more in free love and as a writer concerned himself with themes related to sexual problems. (Venus conjunction Uranus and Moon.)

In contrast, Fig. 16 shows the cosmogram of a woman. From the conjunction of Sun, Mercury, Jupiter and Venus a happy love life may be concluded. But Saturn and Uranus form a square to this complex. After the birth of two children, the marriage was disrupted by the death of the husband in an accident. The further course of her life was marked by disappointment, with the exception of some few happy times, and this is traceable back to the conjunction of Moon with Neptune (Moon = woman, Neptune = disappointment, hence disappointed woman).

One man whose natal chart had Sun trine Moon but also at the same time square Uranus got married twice in succession. The main reason for disharmony was his frequent absence from home on many business trips.

Sun square Neptune in one case corresponded to the premature death of the fiancé and to a whole series of disappointments

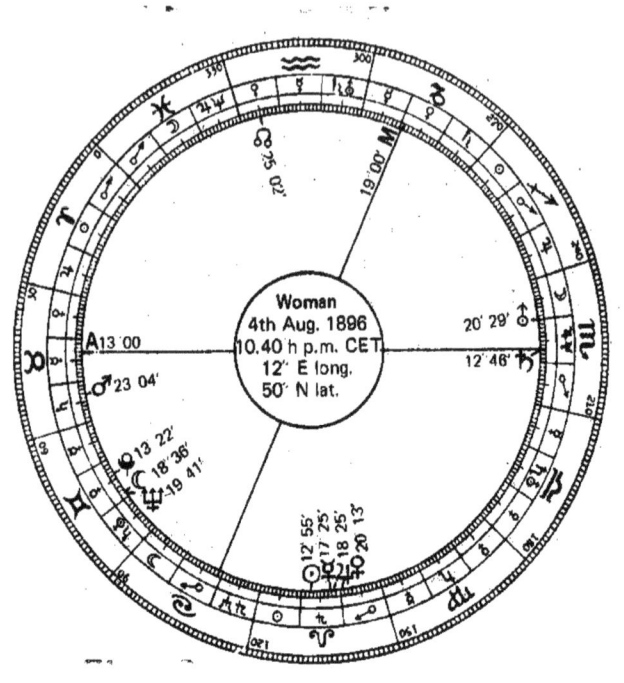

Figure 16

which followed. In another case, a marriage was very unhappy through Sun square Neptune, the husband was a heavy drinker.

The Sun in Virgo is indicative of a negative and magnetic tense introvert with a love of orderliness, power of discrimination, good logic, systematic thinking, exactness, alertness, manual skill, conservatism, good common sense, thoroughness, rationality, tenacity, objectivity, intelligence, good powers of observation, but also pedantry, spirit of contradiction, indecisiveness. These individuals are modest, reliable, formal, unpretentious, discreet, thrifty, industrious, constant, assiduous, also frequently nervous, reserved, insincere, timid, moody, unsatisfied, prudish. Less developed natures are narrow-minded and strait-laced, tightfisted, fault-finding, quarrelsome, and individuals at a higher level of development are modest, reserved, domestic, model personalities. The men are usually very dutiful and do their work with great objectivity and seriousness, but they tend to dictate to their wives in small things. The women are tidy and diligent housewives, who know how to invest every penny properly and who always have something in reserve.

The Virgo-born see their goal in life to be faithfulness to the smallest detail, but they often neglect to keep the overall view of things in mind. To complement their character, they need a partner who teaches others to be more generous, to expand their horizon, and to tolerate the opinions and judgments of others. Those who cannot escape their pettiness will at times be in a position to drive their partner crazy.

Many Virgo types find it difficult to make the decision to get married, because their critical eye is always on the watch for faults and overlooks a person's good points. Female Virgos therefore are eager to take up a profession, without however fully doing without a love life. Many times, they will marry a second time after their first union has broken up in disappointment; this second union is often happier.

In Fig. 17, Sun is over the Ascendant with the trend toward the subordination of external influences trine to Moon, and here we may presume that the wife has the stronger hand in the marriage. Saturn square Moon, however, is to be regarded as unfavorable and results in the divorce of the first marriage. The second marriage turned out to be very harmonious. A typical example of the disappointment in the first marriage is contained in the conjunction of Venus and Mars in the sign Libra, which often leads to precipitate marriages as a result of strong physical attraction and sexuality, but the mutual affection lessens when the first delirious phase has passed. The danger of separation is

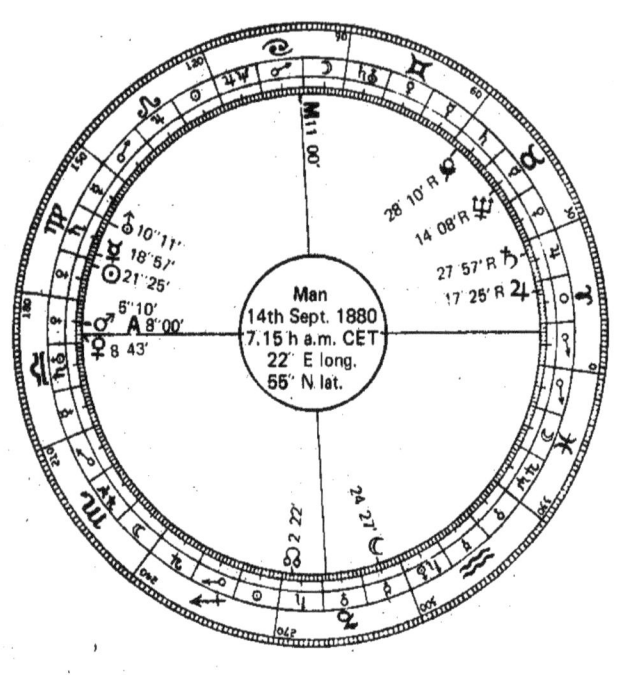

Figure 17

even greater when at the same time the partner also has Venus and Mars conjoined. The native was formerly a civil servant, but became a doctor on inner conviction, a tendency often stimulated by Sun in the sign of Virgo, since Virgo-born are very much concerned with questions of health. A characteristic attribute of the modest Virgoan can be seen in his only demanding one mark for every treatment he gave; he also gave advice to a great number of people free of charge, although, in his learned and competent capacity, he certainly could have been more demanding. His sense of fairness is mirrored in the fact that he treated his children out of both first and second marriages all the same and made no differences.

In another case, a male cosmogram had Sun square Neptune, Moon in Scorpio square Mars, Venus in Cancer square Uranus. The first marriage was unhappy, and a divorce was obtained after much strife. The second appears to be a harmonious one.

The Sun in Libra, i.e. in that sector of the zodiac ruled by Venus, the planet of love, is almost always an indication of rich experience in the realm of love and marriage. These individuals apparently have the inherent ability to give a great deal of love, as well as to gain a lot of experience in love. Unfortunately, the intensity of the momentary attraction does not always go along with a similar degree of constancy, so that there is a marked propensity for affairs on the side. These are electrically and magnetically polarized relaxed extroverts who make contacts readily, who show a love of nature and appreciation of art and beauty, who are alert, open and receptive, enthusiastic, amiable, obliging, natural in behavior, warm-hearted, entertaining, elastic, self-sufficient, adaptive, pliant, communicative, confident, but also inconsiderate, self-righteous, negligent, vain, conceited, complacent, and sweet-toothed. Librans are rarely indebted to their own selves for their position in life, but rather they need the right kind of partner who will provide them with the needed acknowledgment and promotion. The housewives are desirous of making their homes attractive and often shape their environment artistically, whereby they tend to overlook the dust in the corners, and they often spend more money on cosmetics than on the household. The male Librans especially have to be encouraged to show their faithfulness and constancy, mainly in cases where the husband is compelled by business to be away from home on trips. In one marriage, both partners were Librans. The husband did a great deal of traveling and had many opportunities for affairs; the wife took advantage of her husband's frequent absence to play music with a friend of the family, and it was more or less inevitable that more than just a love of music united them. Librans, therefore, should be able to depend on their marital partner to give them firm support, so that no third person can intrude and disrupt their harmony. For their contentment these individuals need an attentive partner who can offer a certain degree of comfort and luxury, aspects of life very much welcomed by the Libran type. Pettiness is a very rare characteristic of these individuals, although there are certainly enough occasions where a bit of pedantry would go a lot farther than liberality.

Fig. 18 shows the cosmogram of a man who lived very happily with his wife to an old age, who at the age of fifty was just as much in love with his wife as a honeymooner. We find here Venus exactly on the midpoint of Sun and Jupiter, the corresponding interpretation in the CSI is: "A healthy love-relationship, a harmonious sex-life . . . the happily loving husband. No matter how happy they are with one another, they still suffer from the lack of children, a result of Neptune's opposition to Venus in Scorpio, this means disappointment (Neptune) in sexual (Scorpio) love (Venus). However, the lunar trine to Saturn and Sun is favorable. Significant is also the fact that Saturn is retrograde and will progressively reach the midpoint Sun/Moon only when death severs the marital union.

The Sun in Scorpio inculcates in the individual the desire and aim to penetrate the material with the spirit, to overcome and become independent of the material. Seen in this connection, it is understandable that the Scorpio-born manifest in a very clear form the various stages of development. They are often too much tied up in material things to be able to extricate themselves with any ease. These individuals cannot be blamed when their tireless activity, unlimited perseverance and energy, their tenacity in going after their ends and utmost exertion of energy come to the fore. This excess of energy makes it possible for them to squander the most valuable energy reservoirs of the body and to be tempted to exploit and despoil the body.

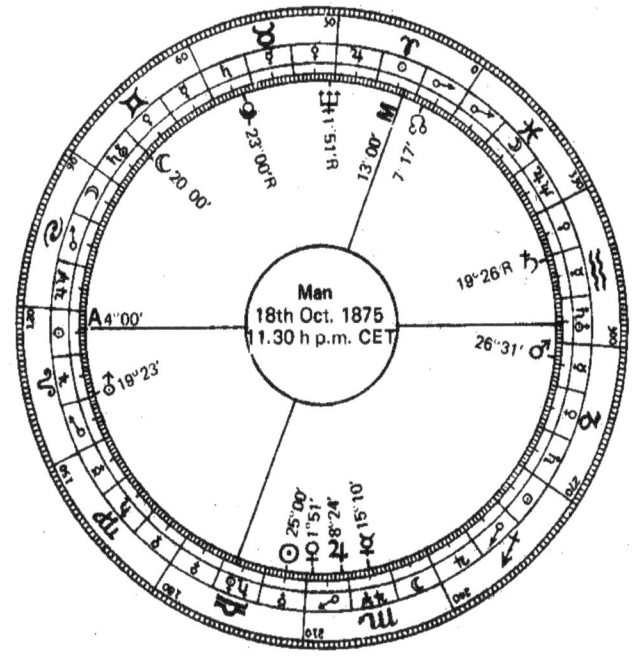

Figure 18

These are tense introverts possessing physical activeness, practical sense, skill, thoroughness, love of independence, self-assurance, reflectiveness, impressionability, impenetrableness, great sensuality, cynicism and enmity in dealing with others. These types are self-sufficient, industrious, deep, principled, willing to sacrifice, but also obstinate, defiant, rated too high in their own self-esteem, withdrawn, ruthless, quick-tempered, vindictive, moody, vulgar, seductible, resentful, and very jealous.

Both the men and the women have to restrain their passion, to keep sensual pleasure from triumphing over true love.

These individuals are, however, nearly always reliable and pursue their aims with zeal. They require of their partner absolute dedication and are easily aroused when things are not going their way. However, this does not keep them from being particularly friendly and warm-hearted the very next moment. Scorpio-born are constantly trying to keep themselves under control and to have the upper hand over their instinctual and emotional life, and to transform instinctual energy into creative force.

It is especially difficult to find the right kind of complementation for these individuals, because, on the one hand, the partner has to be pretty thick-skinned in order to be able to stand up to the "Scorpion bites," and on the other hand, he must also act as a compensating factor and provide firm moral and ethical support. There is the inherent danger of becoming unfaithful, of going morally astray or of falling into inner rigidity.

Early marriage is advisable for these individuals, in order for them to find the right kind of compensation in their life-long partners.

Fig. 19 has the cosmogram of a man who described his marriage, there were four children, as very happy. Moon in trine to Jupiter is typical for happy relations (Jupiter) with the wife (Moon). Jupiter at MC is indicative of an individual who is successful in his vocation and who consequently is able to offer his family something. Sun opposition Mars and Venus opposition Saturn have no doubt brought up some crisis or other in the course of this marriage, but which, thanks to the right mate and his own stability of character, could be overcome. This example shows that it is not absolutely imperative to give in to the disposition mapped out by the cosmogram, but that it is possible to an extent to work on and improve oneself. Marriages with many children are very seldom found with individuals having Sun in

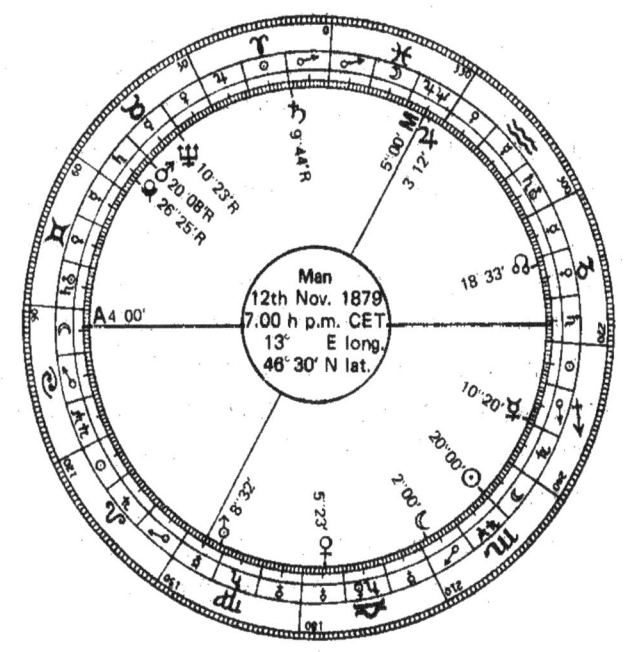

Figure 19

Scorpio, since many of them consider the fulfillment of passion to be more important than the desire for children. In many cases, this is connected with the desire first to lay the groundwork of security before thinking of starting a family.

Occasionally, one may find among the Scorpio-born the very opposite attitude. On the one hand, they demand fulfillment of their sensual and material desires, often involving a large amount of ruthlessness, and on the other, they are deeply religious and interested in all philosophical questions, and this on a very high intellectual plane, quite in contrast to the other side of their character. This is expressed in the cosmogram of a man having Sun in Scorpio square Moon. An unfavorable combination of Sun and Moon generally indicates a conflict between volition and capability, between wish and reality, between obligation and inclination. This man immersed himself in intellectual problems and could give other people the best of advice, but was himself not able to keep up his marriage, and after the divorce made such demands as cannot possibly be fulfilled in this day and age.

We hardly need mention that the statistics on Scorpio individuals contain very many cases in which there is involvement in the lowest and oldest profession.

The Sun in Sagittarius applies to the electric and positive, tense extrovert, who possesses good intuition, is creative, goal-conscious, far-seeing, exuberant, bold; he has good powers of observation, organizational flair, urge for independence, presence of mind, but he also tends to be imprudent, fickle, and superficial. In his relations with others he is prone to be enthused, self-satisfied, ambitious, eager, animated, independent, enterprising, circumspect, proud, dignified, class-conscious, but also at times conceited, obtrusive, boastful, arrogant, pretentious, reckless, and a lover of comfort and ease. Men and women both can be very animated, outgoing and jolly. Sagittarians are prone to go after high ideals but are susceptible to severe disappointment when they don't allow enough time for the attainment of their goals or give up their pursual prematurely due to impatience.

The mental agility of these individuals makes them especially fond of an exchange of ideas and seek satisfaction for their thirst for knowledge; their physical agility keeps them on the outlook for activity, either vocationally or physically. Socially, they enjoy being "the life of the party." Jollity can easily turn to wantonness, frankness does not always keep within the proper bounds, precipitancy leads to error. These are characteristics which often provide the groundwork for differences with the partner. Regrettably, outsiders are often confided in, instead of discussing the matters in question with members of the family.

According to the rules of traditional astrology, Sagittarians are generally supposed to marry twice. The reason for this could be that they tend to enter a union prematurely and without proper consideration, and the consequence is bound to be disappointment. These individuals need a partner who can give them sound, moral support and who has the same interests, so that leisure time can be spent together; otherwise, there is the danger that the Sagittarian—like the Gemini-born—will go his own separate way and will choose another sports partner, dancing partner or kindred spirit in the arts.

The Sagittarians especially love harmony, a cosy home and a generous life style; they enjoy making plans, adore their beloved and rave about their happiness.

A native born in December 1901 (Fig. 20) described his marriage (the wedding took place April 25, 1931) as follows: "Since our wedding day we have been one in body and soul. We've never been able to be apart more than 24 hours. Our love becomes deeper and our soul union stronger and happier every day." Only a Sagittarian could write like this. His wife was born April 25, 1914, and there are some very good aspects connecting them such as Sun trine Mars, Moon trine Mars, Venus trine Venus etc., although Neptune and Mars opposition Venus present them with many a test. The basic configuration is peculiar. Jupiter and Saturn are jointly located between Venus and Mars, so that the happy (Jupiter) instinctual life (Venus/Mars) is also subjected to inhibition or disruption (Saturn).

A native born October 21, 1899 judged his Sagittarian wife, born November 28, 1901 (exact time is unfortunately not

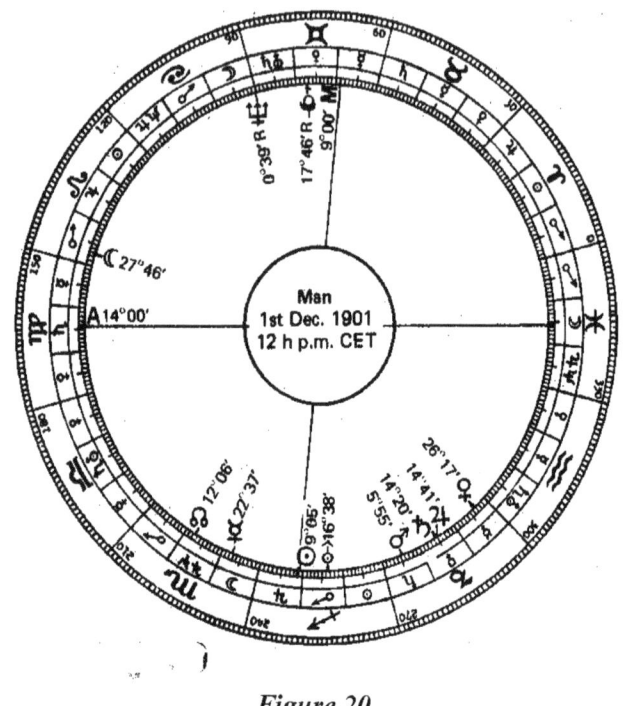

Figure 20

known) very severely; they were married February 1, 1929. "This marriage, which was almost fatal for me, only lasted six months. My ex-wife was interested in skiing and in dancing, was unfaithfulness in persona, a pathological liar, and was hysterical and materialistic. Before our marriage, she acted the part of an unhappy, unassuming, God-fearing woman, and she was very convincing. I thought this woman would be better able to handle the material things than I and would cheer me up. I might also add that erotically we got along with each other very well, but this is not sufficient basis for a marriage." (Fig. 21) This woman was born only a few days before the man in the above example, and we find here the same configuration of Jupiter and Saturn on the midpoint of Venus/Mars, but with the addition of

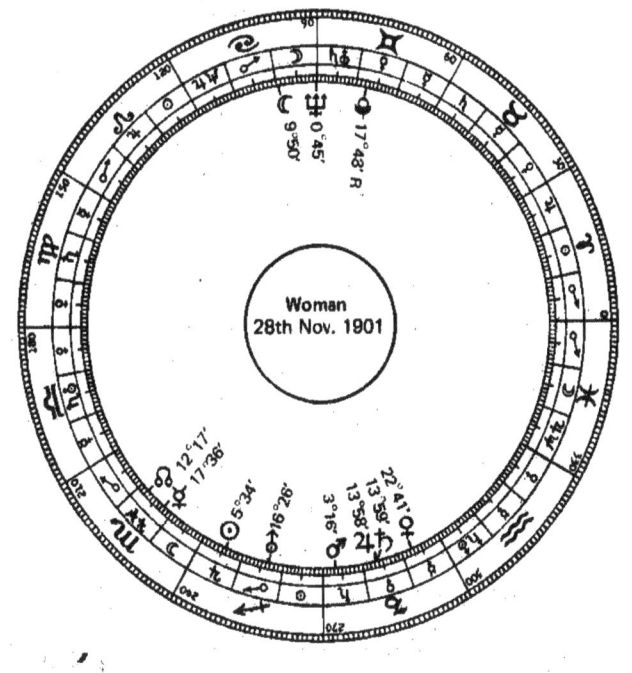

Figure 21

the lunar opposition. The Moon is located here in its own sign, Cancer, and Saturn is in its own sign, Capricorn. ("Own sign" is given to mean that sign ruled by the stellar body in question, e.g. where there is a certain relationship, as is the case between Moon and Cancer and between Saturn and Capricorn.) This lunar opposition was not present in the foregoing example, instead the Moon was square Mercury, which is of little significance for a life partnership. Aside from this, the first example shows Ascendant in a harmonious trine to Jupiter and Saturn. Unfortunately, the hour of birth is not known for the second example.

The following was told about a single woman born December 3, 1893: "Up until her 33rd year of life the native was pretty much favored by fortune, especially so in the period between the ages of 20 to 33. She had a large circle of friends and acquaintances where-over she went, even though she was a rather quiet type. She always wanted to get married and had many an opportunity to do so, but nothing ever came of it. Either she herself abruptly broke off the relationship, because she for some indefinite reason or another felt she couldn't marry the man in question, or the man was already tied down. At the age of 33, a very bad time in every respect began for the native." (Fig. 22).

The Sun is located in the sign of Sagittarius, indicating on the one hand her ability to make ready contact with others and on the other hand her divided personality characterized by indecisive-ness especially due to Neptune's opposition to Sun, which is in itself an indication of disappointment (Neptune) regarding men. Moon conjunction Saturn in the sign of Libra and additionally opposition Moon's Node contributed to the breaking-up (Saturn) of the relationships (Moon's Node), whereby the woman (Moon) remained single (Saturn). From Mars conjunction Uranus in Scorpio we may conclude some organic disorders. That she nevertheless had a large circle of friends can be traced back to Venus trine Jupiter. The critical configurations still were stronger and in no way promoted happiness (Jupiter) in love (Venus).

The Sun in Capricorn always reminds one that duty and obligation are in first place, that every task should be carried out conscientiously. that goals should be pursued with perseverance and patience, that one's ambitions should be fulfilled and recognition attained. Thrift, quiet solitude and a simple way of living help to bring about satisfaction and success in life, even when success is not always easily attainable. These are "negative and magnetic introverts", who have to digest every experience and impression inwardly and who need time before they can make a decision, which, however, they will carry out with

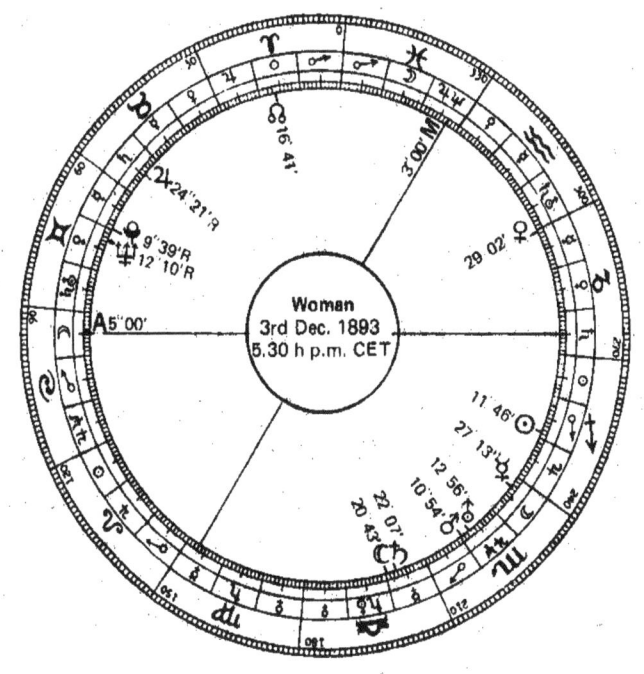

Figure 22

great determination. They are characterized by firmness, patience, principle, methodical ness, objectivity, clear-headedness, tenacity, common sense, formative urge, acumen, moderation, and the power of concentration. They are firm in character, exact, industrious, active, conscientious, efficient, reliable, trustworthy, loyal, independent, discreet and reticent, at times even somewhat inhibited and unsociable. It is not an easy thing for them to establish contact with others. By no means are the Capricorns always the pensive melancholies they are purported to be, they can also be very joyful and happy, witty and full of good humor, and very sharp-witted. However, they first need a certain time of adjustment to the environment before they can really open up. They tend to be impenetrable to others and like to reserve their opinions, they are inclined to coolness of demeanor, hiding a wealth of emotion; they are capable of passion, but will rarely show the extent of their heart's glow. They take life very seriously and enjoy grappling with difficult problems, and at times look into the future more pessimistically than need be. They are very dutiful and loyal and will always be endeavored to keep a marriage intact, no matter what. Of course, these main characteristics may be intensified or altered by the other configurations contained in the natal chart.

A woman born January 18, 1884 was separated form her husband, but continued to stand by and help him, despite the suffering he had caused her. She wrote in a letter: "For months now, he's been moving in very dubious and inferior circles and associates with certain elements he used to be repelled by. He's also started to drink. The only thing I could do to help him has been to withdraw my suit for divorce on the day of its decree. Inwardly convinced that it would be better to deprive myself of my ultimate rights in order to be able to stand by him in case of dire need, since his friends and his perverse girl-friend are only taking advantage of him. I have been very bitter for a long while, because I really have loved my husband and suffered greatly because of him. We've been married nineteen years, and I guess my husband has always been complaining and petty, as the Virgoans usually are (September 2, 1891, 3:00 a.m.). But morally he had always been completely upright, now he's the opposite. Even though my relations only shake their heads over my act and think I lack strength of character, I still think I've done the right thing. I feel it's my duty to stick to my husband, in case he needs someone. . . ." (Fig. 23).

The loyalty, sense of duty and conquest of self evidenced here are characteristic of Sun in Capricorn. These characteristics are intensified through Saturn trine Mercury (and Sun) as well as through Moon trine Saturn. In addition, however, Saturn is lo-

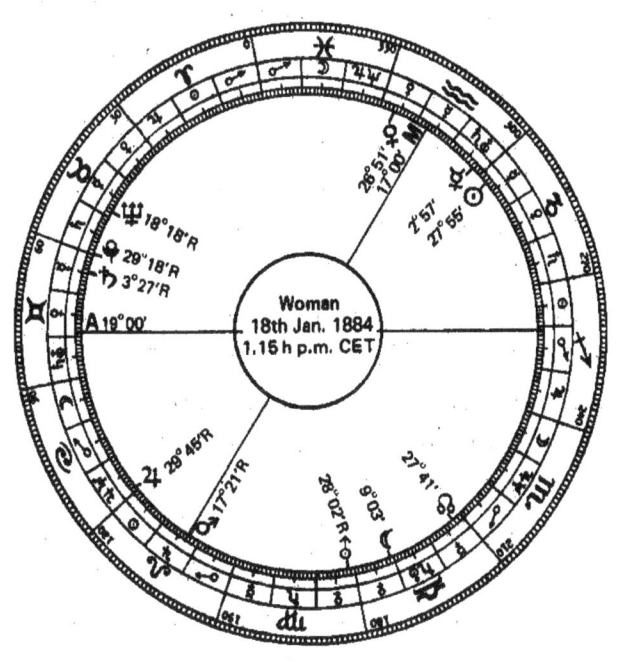

Figure 23

cated almost on the midpoint of Sun and Moon, designating marital (Sun/Moon) difficulties (Saturn). Saturn/Neptune square Venus is indicative of a cooling down and becoming sober and of disappointment, whereas Venus trine Moon's Node and Moon's Node centered between Sun and Jupiter help in keeping the union intact.

The idea of loyalty may be all too narrowly defined by the Capricorn and jealousy overly cultivated, to the extent that it represents a torment for the marital partner. The basic cause of this jealousy may be seen to lie in the desire to uphold the marriage at all costs. These individuals may be able to forgive an act of unfaithfulness but are much less liable to forget. This striving to keep the marriage untainted can imbue in the partner the necessary moral support to avoid any kind of extramarital escapade.

Capricorns do not always get married solely for reasons of love, there are often other considerations involved as well. Many feel their loneliness, others want to escape their parental home because they feel misunderstood, others want to pursue a life's goal with a professional colleague, others see in marriage the possibility to attain a higher station in life through their partner and thus to enhance their own self-importance. Parents and relations frequently do not agree to the marriage or subsequent difficulties may arise later from this end. Individuals with Sun in Capricorn often marry partners considerably older than themselves. A man born February 6, 1884, married a woman born January 18, 1899. Despite the age difference of 15 years, the marriage, after ten years' duration, was regarded as very harmonious.

In another case, a great difference in age turned out to be unfavorable. A woman born on January 15, 1876, married a man born March 25, 1861. The marriage was described as follows: "In the first few months, the marriage went along harmoniously enough. Marital conflicts soon arose which were due for the most part to the wife. In their quarrels, the husband was the more reserved by far of the two (Sun in Pisces!). Suspicion and distrust became more and more part of her now frequent accusation and reproaches against her husband. In these verbal battles, her completely unjustified anxieties about the testament and the inheritance dominated. The odd thing to be observed here is that after her fears in this respect could be allayed by the setting down of the testament in court she raised yet other objections from which could be seen that the fulfillment of these new wishes would not make the marriage any more harmonious either. In these quarrels, the wife showed little love of truth or

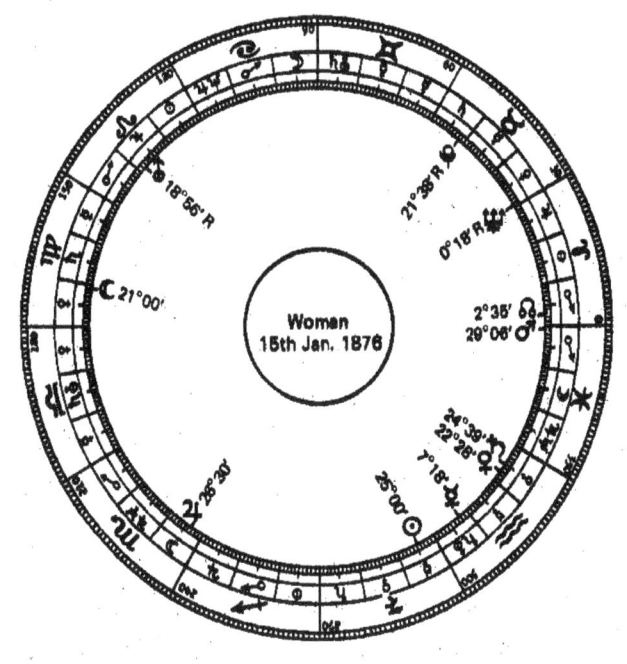

Figure 24

logic and all the more a desire to dominate. Although the marriage has not been separated. . . ." (Fig. 24).

The solar position in Capricorn is not the only factor responsible for the wife's behavior, also involved is Neptune square Sun and Mercury, resulting in the wife's seeing her husband (Sun) in the wrong light (Neptune). In addition, the Neptune square is located at the midpoint of Sun/Mercury, and the CSI[7] states: "The tendency to simulate and to deceive oneself." We also find Venus in conjunction with Saturn and in opposition to Uranus, so that tensions (Uranus) must need result from a coming down to earth (Saturn) with regard to love (Venus). Jupiter trine Mars is favorable in influence, whereas Jupiter square Saturn, Venus and Uranus typifies the difficulties. It must be assumed that the husband's being older by some years required certain sacrifices of the wife and was a cause of her dissatisfaction, non-adjustment and irritability. Whereas on the one hand Saturn conjunction Venus represses passionateness, this is reawakened on the other hand by Uranus opposition Venus repeatedly. The English astrologer Carter[9] says this about Uranus opposition Venus: "that cooperation of any sort becomes impossible. Obstinacy is present and some times an extraordinary rigidity of attitude and opinion from which the native is unable to free himself. With all the unreasonableness of the Uranian, he is not to be moved toward any concession or to yield his standpoint . . ." If we add to this disposition those characteristics adhering to Sun in Capricorn of pertinacity and inflexibility, the result is a personality with whom it is not at all easy to get along.

The Capricorn's life and marital destiny are not always easy, but if the Capricorn-born survive their struggles and they can succeed in overcoming the difficulties facing them, they are just the individuals who could provide a foundation for an indissoluble union.

The Sun in Aquarius designates the relaxed extroverts who are electrically and positively polarized, who are full of ideas and reformative notions to change the environment. They exhibit mental activeness, foresight, ingenuity, quick comprehension, intuition, organizational flair, good sense of humor and fun, sharp-wittedness, and common sense, eloquence, initiative, powers of observation, knowledge of human nature. They are very congenial, but also revolutionary and changeable, full of the desire for reform, visionary, energetic, industrious, cautious, fresh, zealous, mobile, natural, confident, love change, are communicative, generous, but often incalculable, imprudent, prying, superficial, forgetful. These individuals are usually ahead of the times and need a partner who is also able to put a halt in time to hastiness and lack of deliberation. In questions of love, these individuals take no heed or origins or money, instead they bring with them a great deal of idealism, even if a solid financial basis is lacking and there is no prospect for one in the future. Love is for them the understanding of souls, the immersion of I in Thou. Their relations with others, too, are characterized by understanding and a willingness to help, without ever receiving thanks. If at times this obligingness does go too far, the partner is justified in putting a damper on this urge. The men are often idealists, visionaries, or even revolutionists, who are prone to place themselves above more conservative philosophies and the rules of custom. The women are a more impractically-minded kind of housewife and love changes, as seen in their frequent remodeling of their homes or furniture, etc. they are often extravagant and need a husband who can get them back onto a more sensible track.

Very much depends on the stage of development of the individual in question. The primitive type is extremely interested in all innovations, inventions, reforms, and fashionable extravagances; the more highly developed and spiritual type, however, carries within himself ideas and problems of which his contemporaries are not even aware, let alone ripe enough for. Due to the fact that the Aquarians often have one foot in the future and are about to pull the other out of the past, they are often not easy to understand and may create a scandal when they want to do away with out-dated forms of convention or ruthlessly stand up for the truth. The real Aquarian cannot be dissuaded from pursuing his idea or goal, he does not give up his endeavor, but he will admit to himself that he cannot always keep on battering his head against a brick wall, and that a modicum of restraint is necessary for the ripening of an idea or project. The love of these individuals is rooted more in the spiritual and less in the physical and emotional realm, so long as other configurations do not contradict this disposition.

One very happy marriage was that between a man born February 11, 1874, and a woman born August 19, 1875. A peculiar fact is that the husband has four bodies—Saturn, Venus, Sun, Mercury—in Aquarius, and the wife likewise four—Uranus, Venus, Mercury, Sun—but in Leo. This again goes to show that the appearance of oppositions in a synastry do not necessarily have to be unfavorable to the course of a marriage, but rather represent a complementation. An important consideration here, however, is the presence of a great number of harmonious aspects. Very remarkable is the conjunction in the husband's natal chart of Sun and Venus, and this configuration is again formed on the day of the wedding.

A glance at the statistics on the marriages of the Aquarian-born tells us that many unions fail because of a lack of understanding, whereby, of course, the other configurations are also very directly involved, e.g. Saturn formed an unfavorable aspect to Sun. One married woman, an artist, suffered a lot under the economic limitations imposed upon her through her marriage, probably without ever realizing that especially the Aquarian only becomes mature through struggle in order then to be able to carry out his ideas. In her case. Sun and Moon were square, so that she lived in conflict not only with herself, but also with her parents and spouse, with whom she had many differences of opinion.

Many Aquarians enter into several relationships before they find the right partner for life. For them, the marriage ceremony is usually only a formality, gone through for the sake of the partner since they are convinced that true love suffers from externals. Aquarian artists are often of the conviction that a free union can be of higher moral value than a love relationship grounded in civil formalities. These individuals are very occupied, indeed, with questions of love and marriage and often develop viewpoints which are generally not acceptable to most.

The Sun in Pisces corresponds to the "magnetic and negative, relaxed introverts, who are contemplative and impressionable, who possess a great deal of phantasy and imagination, who are lovers of art and music, who are often rather irresolute, negligent and indolent, who seldom make decisions of their own volition and whose attitude on the whole is a passive one. They do not have much self-confidence, are reticent, sensitive, inconstant, anxious, seductible, self-underrating. They are, however, capable of very much love and can even sacrifice themselves for others, and are able to work without demanding recognition for it. These individuals, therefore, need an active partner who gives them support and can pull them along.

The women are often negligent about their household and in their easygoing way will overlook the dust in the corners. Seldom are the men able to assert themselves to the full and advance only slowly in their profession, unless other factors are involved in the natal chart which indicate recognition and success. They can, however, make suitable husbands for women who are more positive-thinking and who prefer "wearing the pants in the family."

Despite a certain inclination for reticence they are very sociable and, in company, can become very talkative and open, whereby alcohol or suchlike will do much to promote this tendency to loosen the tongue.

It is not always easy to assess the real character of these individuals, since they are apt to represent something other than what they truly are. Also, they like having their secrets without, however, there being any ulterior motives involved.

The expression "cold as a fish" is not an inapt description with respect to passionateness. At any rate, the more temperamental partners of Pisceans have complained about their lack of passion. which usually has to kindled. They often love comfort and quiet above all. Therefore, the partner who will "wake them up" is the complement proper to them. Our investigations of the cosmograms of married couples showed the interesting fact that the partners of Pisceans often have Sun in the "fiery signs" (Aries, Leo, Sagittarius), so that the choleric temperament seems to be the best complement for the phlegmatic type.

Marital conflicts often have their origins in the Piscean thinking too little of himself and his loved one and being prepared to make sacrifices for the common good, universal love being more important to him than the love for individuals, or in the case of the more highly developed types increasing spiritualization is paralleled by prematurely decreasing passionateness, and in the case of the more primitive, in the inclination to negligence, to irresponsible acts and secret associations, which can disrupt the marital bond, and in the constant necessity for the negative attitude to be "shaken up" by the partner. It has been determined statistically that individuals with Sun in the sign of Pisces often marry twice. The primary reasons for divorce were unfaithful ness, eccentricities, and many times religious conflicts. In a whole series of cases, disappointment led to complete seclusion, even entrance into a cloister.

A man born March 15, 1882, married to a woman born April 17, 1887, incurred a great number of losses in life, his wife, too, lost her fortune due to war and inflation, but he is still able to manage. His wife, an Arian, is very energetic, industrious, faithful, and works hard to help him, so that the Arian woman is the best complement for the Piscean man. In the report made on the marriage after 26 years, the husband merely mentioned that his wife was a bit suspicious as far as love was concerned. The husband, however, is very much attached to his wife and would like the marriage to continue. Sun conjunction Venus and Moon trine Jupiter are especially favorable factors in his natal chart (Fig. 25).

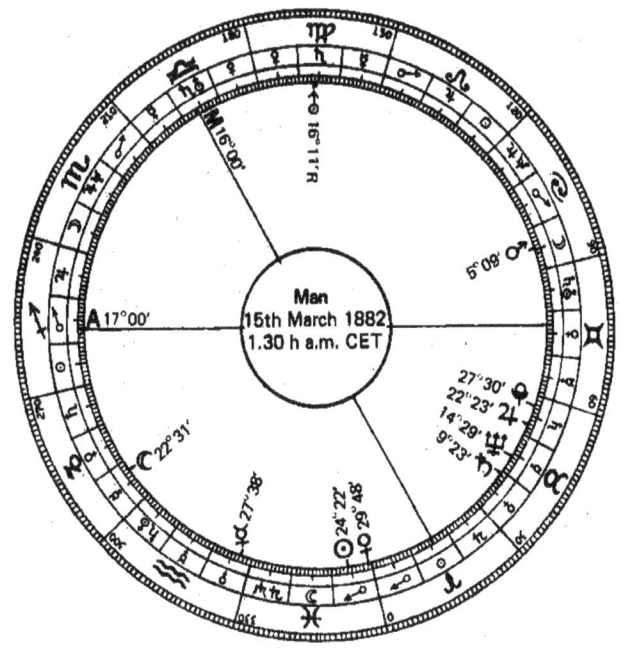

Figure 25

A woman says this about a particularly unfortunate marriage: "I was born on March 6, 1871, 10:52 a.m., in M.. Upper Bavaria. My husband was born on March 27, 1870. We first met at the end of October 1890, at a parish fair. We were married on October 16, 1897. It was an unhappy marriage; we had two children, our son was born November 24, 1898, 5:00 a.m., our daughter April 21, 1903, 13:30 a.m. I am very attached to my children, but they have withdrawn themselves from me, my daughter completely, my son has been terribly brutal and unkind to me. He sometimes comes around, but I can expect nothing from my children despite my need. The divorce, where I was given custody of the children because of my attachment to them, was decreed on January 10, 1910. Since then I have been living all

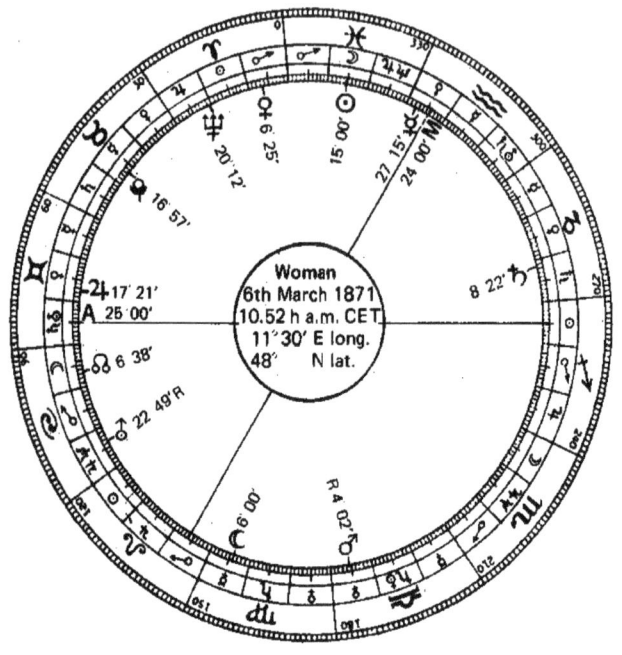

Figure 26

alone and have absolutely no contact with others and have been unable to find any. I am interested in spiritual and intellectual endeavors, after all one must have some interest in life. . . ." (Fig. 26).

Sun and Moon are located in opposing signs, which should generally be considered as unfavorable. Venus square Saturn indicates a cooling down of love, and Saturn opposition Moon's Node points to separation. Saturn square to Mars is somewhat allayed by Saturn trine Moon. The following can be termed a characteristic planetary picture: Saturn and Moon's Node are located on the axis of Venus and Mars, which the CSI interprets as follows: "Sex union. Inhibitions in love-life, a separation in love." Venus and Mars are at the midpoint of Sun/Neptune: "A weakened or disturbed sex-life, disappointments, aberrations in love or sex-expression." The square of Sun to Jupiter cannot be regarded as quite so critical, the other configurations being decisive for the unhappy marriage. As we can see, one may not rely solely on the solar position, but rather the cosmogram as a whole must be considered.

The Moon in the Signs of the Zodiac

The Moon designates—to give a few keywords—the negative, the feminine, the imperfect, the fleeting, the personal, the inconstant, the spiritual. In the female natal chart, the Moon represents the I. in the male chart the Thou; with women, the Moon relates to the pro-creative organs. In any case, the Moon provides insight into emotional disposition and spiritual contactability. (Comprehensive discussions on the Moon in the natal chart are contained in books of interpretation.)

Moon in Aries is an indication that emotion and feeling are at the root of actions and decisions. This individual acts impulsively and prematurely, and is in the moment of his zeal not to be kept back or dissuaded, he is very hard to divert from his goals, and is often subject to overestimation of self. In love, individuals with Moon in Aries are quickly inflamed and enthusiastic, ready to do battle in order to win the heart of the beloved and to persuade and convince through the depth of their feeling and passion. Objective considerations are easily disregarded in his endeavor to "make a conquest." A marriage is often contracted precipitantly; once the goal has been attained, a sobering-up period usually follows. Whichever one of the partners has Moon in Aries will gladly do the managing in the marriage. In the male natal chart. Moon in Aries points to a very energetic wife, to whom a more negatively-minded husband will tend to subordinate himself. A woman with Moon in Aries wants a husband whom she can look up to and for whose affection she is willing to fight. If there are difficulties in the way of realizing certain goals, the struggle will not be abandoned, even if it seems to be hopeless due to one partner already being obligated to another, as an extreme case.

A man born August 14, 1889, at 4:30 p.m. in Cologne, in whose cosmogram the Moon is located not only in Aries but also in a trine to Mars in Leo, had an allegedly harmless affair with a married woman, which lasted for three years without any disturbance. In spite of legal difficulties which came later, in spite of the woman's repeated attempts to discourage him, in spite of proof of unfaithfulness and the birth of an illegitimate child, which was the grounds for the divorce from her first husband, this man still continued to pursue this woman with his love.

A woman born June 15, 1906, who had in her natal chart Moon in Aries square to Uranus and Neptune, married a man born August 12, 1900, whose cosmogram had Moon in Pisces trine to Venus, but also square to Uranus. The woman wrote about her marriage: "We both had pretty nearly the same way of thinking, but my husband is very reserved (Pisces), so that our marriage is not really as I imagined it would be. I have the feeling I'm not really what he wants. Nevertheless, I have no real cause for complaint, since he is very steady and reliable." Here the differences in character due to the lunar positions become very obvious. On the whole, this should not necessarily be unfavorable. However, Saturn in the sign of Pisces in the woman's natal chart is located very nearly in the same position as the man's Moon, whereas, in addition, the woman's Sun is located at 23° Gemini in opposition to the man's Saturn at 28° Sagittarius. This means there are mutual inhibitions which have to find release if genuine understanding is to come about. It is understandable that the wife, with Moon in Aries, would like to be the guiding hand in the marriage, whereby the husband, with Sun in the sign of Leo, by no means intends to have the reins taken out of his hands.

A man born February 6, 1884, after ten years of marriage to a woman born January 18, 1899, called it harmonious. The female Moon is located in Aries, the male Moon in Gemini. Moon trine Sun in the husband's cosmogram make for a compensating and harmonious disposition, which knows how to be accommodating and can mediate in critical situations.

In many cases, the fighting characteristics as dictated by the lunar position in Aries are often very necessary indeed in order to keep the marriage alive and to meet the costs of living. There is the case of a woman, whose Moon was located in Aries, married to a man who was ailing in health and who died of pneumonia after only a few years of marriage. The woman was compelled not only to take over the management of the household but also to take her husband's place in his business and carry out all his directions. The marriage was very happy despite his illness, because the wife was able to make full use of her "Arian energy."

Moon in Taurus makes for deep and long lasting feeling, combined with strong but controlled passion. These individuals, somewhat conservative in their attitudes and life-style, require the most quiet and regular life possible along with the consistent adherence to their principles and goals in life. Despite their emotionally directed attitude their useful and practical sides still come very strongly to the fore. Ambition, too, wants its fulfillment. Congeniality will win many friends, but who will tend to take advantage of the goodwill offered them. Thanks, too, to their fidelity and loyalty, these individuals with Moon in Taurus will have many a bad experience, because they take life seriously, and others do not keep their promises. A healthy sensuality (opposition Scorpio!) demands satisfaction, and if this is not attained, slight aberrations in love and marriage are possible. In many cases, the drive for security and financial gain is too predominate.

The following was written about a man born February 13, 1883: "He is somewhat small in stature, but he is tough in nature and will-power. He is very zealous in his work, leaving no room for feelings. On the outside, he is obliging, pious too, but material thoughts keep drowning out everything else." For his wife, this marriage was a "torture." All his letters speak of nothing but money. This materialistic attitude was especially furthered by the position of Saturn also in Taurus, furthermore by the conjunction of Mercury and Mars and square to Moon.

Generally speaking, individuals with Moon in Taurus make good spouses, assuming they have found the right partners, as was the case with one couple, discussed under "Sun in Sagittarius" (Fig. 20). (December 1, 1901 and April 25, 1914.) The wife had her Moon at 8° Taurus, the husband Mars at 5° Capricorn, so that their strong tie had its basis in Moon trine Mars. The one thing that really hurts individuals with Moon in Taurus is being rejected;

they always need recognition. Their emotional experience is very deeply rooted, they find it difficult to forget and are inclined to bear grudges.

Moon in Gemini is indicative of a lively and mediatory character with multiple talents and interests, with an urge for change and diversion, and with fluctuating moods and emotions. Therefore, these individuals need a partner representing a center of calm in the marriage. Inwardly, there are quite a number of conflicts to be resolved. Many conflicts result from the continuance of several relationships at one time and in the difficulty in deciding which partner can be awarded the greater love. Very many friendships are made especially during adolescence, whereby liveliness and sociability are contributing factors. Only when a true inner bond exists between the partners will these individuals be able to remain faithful, otherwise, they are inclined to keep up relationships alongside of their marriage, a fact which can lead to a disruption of the legal bond.

With reference to emotional and sexual life, individuals with Moon in Gemini may be easily excitable, but they never find satisfaction solely in the sensual realm. Once their infatuation has died down, discussion and mutual stimulation are necessary to keep them from straying to others. A woman with Moon in Gemini will show great interest in the affairs of her husband, will want to know how he is doing in his work, and wants to be told a lot about him. Only in this way does she find it possible to bear the lonely hours in her husband's absence. In the same way, a man with a lunar position in Gemini will be greatly interested in his wife's activities and daily experiences, will want to do something constructive for their joint recreation in order to provide her with some diversion from the monotony of the daily routine. A woman who is unable to truly estimate this attitude of her husband and prefers staying at home places the husband in danger of seeking his diversion elsewhere, a possible hazard to the marriage itself.

The position of the Moon in Gemini very much depends on the aspects of the other bodies in the natal chart especially significant. Moon in Gemini trine Sun is contained in the cosmogram of a man who was very happily married. Moon in Gemini trine Uranus has also proved to be favorable. Moon in Gemini square Uranus was termed by one woman as the cause for her unfaithful-ness, which resulted in divorce. Moon conjunction Neptune and Mars in Gemini brought about so many disappointments for one woman that she preferred remaining a career woman and single. In another natal chart. Moon in Gemini in conjunction with Neptune was regarded as responsible for there being many relationships but no decision for marriage. Moon in Gemini opposition Saturn is in the cosmogram of one man who mistreated his wife. (Moon = emotion, Saturn = coldness, hence insensibility.)

Moon in Cancer, i.e. in its "home sign" (Moon = ruler of Cancer), corresponds to a very strong and easily influenced emotional reaction. (Even the state of health is greatly influenced, especially digestion. Moon and Cancer relate to the stomach. Emotional suffering is often expressed by a temporary lack of appetite, stomach pains and cramps, etc.)

Moods change frequently, whereby there is a strong emotional reaction to environmental influences. (Such reactions are felt more emphatically by these individuals than by others because of their inherent sensitivity and susceptibility. Their tears flow more readily as a rule. Their receptiveness is often so pronounced that they are easily able to grasp the thoughts of others and to act accordingly. They therefore require of their partner the greatest consideration for their emotional states, otherwise these "lunar crabs" withdraw into themselves and remain reserved. Hence there is always the danger present that contact may be disrupted through any unconsidered word.

Individuals with Moon in Cancer love a cosy home, are content even in modest circumstances, and are thrifty. The men are usually good husbands and fathers and are happiest when at home.

The women are very capable at giving their environment a harmonious tone and like to mother not only their families but also their guests. Under favorable aspects to the Moon, these individuals are constant and faithful, but under unfavorable aspects they often lack steadfastness and solidity and self-control. Since the Moon "rules" the bodily liquids and is located here in a "watery sign," Cancer, there is usually great thirst, which can turn out to be of disadvantage if this thirst is quenched by alcohol. Individuals with a strong occupation of Cancer often have a connection with restaurants and the like.

A hotel secretary with Moon in Cancer trine Uranus had a number of intimate relationships, but without ever getting married. A man with Moon in Cancer opposition Mars became a drinker, became intimate with the housekeeper and finally was divorced by his wife. A woman with Moon in Cancer square Mercury was married to a restaurant proprietor and suffered a nervous breakdown.

Besides these exceptions, however, there are very many cases where a true inner bond exists between the two partners. A man whose cosmogram contains Moon in Cancer in a trine to Mars was very happily married and could not get over his wife's premature death; he only remarried ten years later, and only because he was compelled by circumstances. A girl with Moon in Cancer trine to Uranus remained faithful to the memory of her fiancé, who was killed in the war, and never married.

Many cases have shown that woman with Moon in Cancer marry men very much their senior who, in addition, had not been happy in their first marriages.

Moon in Leo relates to kindness and open-heartedness, a nature capable of a great deal of love. This rich and warm disposition finds contact everywhere. A love of harmonious companionability, joy of music and art, and enjoyment of stimulating conversation and pleasure all make for general popularity. However, this is often coupled with the difficulty of picking out the right partner from many. Thanks to their self-assurance, authoritative character, their "enchanting" appearance or even extraordinary charm these individuals have a strong power of attraction, which "intoxicates" their partner and robs them of their objectivity. A woman who divorced her husband, who had Moon in Leo in his natal chart, told the following: "When anybody asks me why I ever married this man, I try in vain to recall my emotional state at the time!" Oftentimes, the decisive factor is not the impression made on the prospective partner, but rather that made on the parents-in-law, who may be so enthused about the "imposing man" or the "enchanting woman" that they maneuver their child into the marriage.

Their wide open heart is at times too big to give just one partner all their love, especially when this partner does not equally appreciate social joys and pleasures. The Leo-disposition needs joy and brightness and will by no means be able in the long-run to put up with a pessimistic or prosaic wife. On the other hand, it is necessary for the partner to keep the "lunar lion" within bounds, not only to keep an eye on income and expenditures but also on marital fidelity. Exaggerated good-naturedness and willingness to help can be of disadvantage, as we see in the case of a man who lived in the house of his wife's parents; he gladly placed his entire salary at their disposal, without realizing what actually happened with his money until he one day found out that his mother-in-law, who managed the household, had—thanks to his generosity—very much enlarged her own bank account.

Of decisive significance with the positioning of the Moon in Leo as in other signs are the aspects with the other bodies. A woman with Moon in Leo square Neptune experienced many severe disappointments. Moon trine Venus resulted in one man's case in a rich and varied love-life, since other configurations were an impediment to a marriage.

Moon in Virgo makes the emotional realm subject to the intellect, so that these individuals have difficulty in differentiating between their inner feeling and their expression. Also they are often inhibited in giving their feelings full rein for fear of exposing themselves or revealing their innermost being. However, there are also very many people with this lunar position who regard life solely from a practical and objective standpoint. If they wish to get married, they do not let love alone decide, but rather they subject their prospective partners to a critical review and pay close attention to practical considerations. A woman asks about security, a man is looking for an industrious housewife or hardworking partner in his business. Whereas these individuals are often very pedantic in their estimations and are often inclined to suspicion and mistrust, they are by no means as proper as they give themselves to be and will often say something that does not strictly adhere to the truth. (Confer also the example under "Sun in Capricorn," where Moon in Virgo was present with both of the partners.)

There is much to be said for careful consideration, an objective assessment of circumstances and a well-grounded knowledge of the partner-to-be before marriage is entered into, since this can prevent a hasty marriage and can prove to be of much value for a harmonious life together. It is in no way mere coincidence when such partners are sought and found who also have Moon in Virgo or its trine, in Taurus or Capricorn, since with these individuals joint endeavors and interest go far to promote marital harmony. "My wife and I have a good life together," wrote a man who like his wife has Moon in Virgo in his cosmogram. Another man characterized his marriage as follows: "I have been married twenty-five years. Except for a few little spats our marriage has been harmonious for the most part, but unfortunately we have no children!" The lack of children is occasionally caused by there being at first no desire for children because of the financial situation, and later when the couple has already grown older it is then too late. Since individuals with Moon in Virgo are very fastidious, they often marry very late in life or not at all. With this lunar position, divorces seem to be seldom.

(The reason might be in some cases that a separation is avoided in order not to be exposed to the public eye.)

Moon in Libra makes for a great need for love, because life without a partner would seem empty otherwise. These individuals need a partner who will give meaning to their life, who will give steady support in the struggle for existence and who will keep them on balance. Even when Moon in Libra is favorably aspected, the attitude towards love-life will not always be such that marital harmony will be maintained. The urge for love, awakened early. led in many cases under this lunar position to illegitimate children, but this cannot be considered as the rule. Life is not taken over-seriously, and if fate does strike, it will be overcome fairly readily, since these individuals possess great adaptability in the face of many eventualities. The following letter, written by a woman, is typical: "Despite the great difference in age (husband born April 4, 1880, wife born July 29, 1903) we got along very well with each other. Only one thing makes me a bit sad, the fact that we have no children. We both want children, but this wish has not yet been fulfilled, even though we are both healthy and strong, and my husband, in spite of his 52 years, is still fresh and young-looking. People usually judge his age to be somewhere between 40 and 45. We are both vegetarians, our diet consists almost completely of uncooked food and is very modest. If I knew for sure that we will never have children. I could get over it and apply myself to other interests in life. Till now it has always been my conviction that I need some sort of definite and useful goal in life. Up to now, the best and most useful goal was that of motherhood and the obligations tied up with it. However, if this is not to be my lot, then I will just have to turn to something else, there are after all enough noble and valuable aims worthy of dedication."

This woman, whose natal chart has Moon in Libra has not only managed to live happily with a husband 23 years older than herself (Moon trine Saturn), but would be able to renounce motherhood. In her natal chart Sun and Saturn are in opposition and Uranus and Venus are square, so that some physical disorder is most likely the cause for there being no children. Accordingly, the husband's cosmogram has Saturn conjunction Sun in Aries, and hence similar configurations in both natal charts point to a joint fate.

Moon in Scorpio makes happiness in love greatly dependent on control over sex life. Bad aspects will result in a woman's case especially in abdominal disorders, which do have some influence over the marital life. Usually, character consists more in obstinacy than adaptability, more ruthlessness than tact, more desire for revenge than forgiveness, more one-sidedness than versatility. These individuals find it hard to keep to the middle road and tend much more to extremes. Oftentimes, the dark side of life has to be struggled through before they have control over themselves and passionateness has been subdued to a certain degree, and more ethical or religious goals pursued. A man born June 18, 1891, with Moon in Scorpio trine Mars wrote about himself: "I am the son of a shoemaker, who was a quick-tempered, taciturn, and sensual man. I myself went through a very miserable childhood. My parents' fights and everything else I experienced poisoned me mentally and emotionally: I suffered terribly and was about to go under. It was my marriage which first gave me some order in my life. Only our living conditions are pretty poor despite all the things we do without. I am a non-smoker, anti-alcoholic, and go to no entertainments. . . My children are always ailing. My wife was very ill in 1928 and came home practically a cripple, so that she no longer can play the role of a wife. This is torture for both of us. But I cannot simply abandon my family, I must stay and bear it. I try to find strength in occupying myself with intellectual problems, I fight against my double nature, I look for my better self. . . ."

This confrontation between passionateness and intellectual striving is to be found very often among the Scorpions, who can be very worthy individuals, in fact even superior to and more capable of higher things than those who appear to be better balanced. If the right partner has been found, then love-life can be very harmonious, especially in a marriage blessed with many children.

In the case of men with Moon in Scorpio it has been repeatedly found that their wives are prone to abdominal disorders when the husbands do not have themselves sufficiently under control. The "martian force" of the sign of Scorpio must therefore be transformed into accomplishment elsewhere and ought not to be confined to the erotic realm alone.

Moon in Sagittarius indicates physical as well as mental agility and adaptability, so that individuals having this lunar position in their natal chart will not find it difficult to establish the right kind of relationship to their partner, that is unless the Moon is unfavorably aspected or other configurations are hindrances. A certain degree of conflict in character will make more firmness and stead-fastness necessary in the partner. According to the material at hand, marriages with this lunar position were on the whole good, only where critical aspects put in an appearance did the danger of infidelity become present, whereby usually very much younger persons were the guilty parties.

In order to fulfill the desire for change and diversion, it is good when both partners share the same interests, are active in sports or undertake travels together. If, however, one of the partners suffers from the other's being inhibitory in this respect, then differences are likely to arise, resulting in the possible danger of some third person intervening.

A frequent change of moods should not be taken very seriously. Here, too, very much depends on the partner, who should try to compensate and to check the other's over-exuberance, and to cheer him up when he's feeling depressed.

Moon in Capricorn points to a modest and natural personality. Emotionally, these individuals are not so cool as they are purported to be, instead, they are not always able to express their feelings in the right way, they do not want to reveal their inner life, keep to themselves and try always to appear composed, outwardly at least. They avoid every kind of conspicuousness and for this reason do not indulge in any show of affection.

These individuals highly value a cosy home, are satisfied with a modest life-style, shape their environment on practical principles, feel an inner bond with their homeland and love living on their own ground.

They took for partners who are satisfied with modest circumstances. The men with Moon in Capricorn look for a wife who will be a domestic, practical and economical housewife, they gladly do without a "lady of fashion". If the wife is more generous in her disposition, the husband will pull in the reins and keep a tighter fist on his wallet than perhaps need be. Women with this lunar position are very practically-minded housewives and are happy when their husbands stay at home and indulge themselves in their family. Those men are preferred as life's companions who are considerably older or who are markedly mature and serious.

These individuals are steadfast in love and faithful, they are also very anxious that their partner belongs to them alone. Unfaithfulness on the side of the partner is not easily forgotten, or else the consequences are brought into play right off. A woman physician, whose natal chart had Moon in Capricorn, divorced her husband after only fourteen days of marriage because he had committed adultery.

Due to their inability to express their feelings readily and openly, these individuals tend to continue in their ill-humor for quite awhile, they are very reticent and find it difficult to subject themselves to a talking-out. For this reason, the partner should always take care to allay ill-feeling to stave off greater tensions. The sign of Capricorn has as its "ruler" Saturn, hence Moon in Capricorn is under the influence of Saturn, and the partner has to exert himself to make the other more emotionally inhibiting and depressive partner relaxed and outgoing.

Moon in Aquarius usually makes for a very congenial nature, willingness to help, ability to empathize, as well as a love of independence and freedom, self-sufficiency, self-will, and innovative striving. These individuals find it difficult to accommodate themselves in the long-run, they are unable to take a narrow view on love, instead they tend in some part to a general love of mankind, which, for them, takes precedence over individual love, this standpoint, however, does not necessarily allow for infidelity.

A woman born September 27, 1898 married a man 33 years older than she. This woman was very striking in appearance and possessed good "Libran characteristics," but in contrast the husband was less imposing in character, yet was very nobly-minded. For almost six years, the wife led a double marriage in the very same house before the husband ever noticed anything. She had intended to maintain this status until the death of her husband, especially since he was no longer able to fulfill certain marital duties. But the marriage was immediately divorced on the grounds of adultery. Typifying the situation is the location of Moon in the last degrees of Aquarius in a square to Uranus at the midpoint of Venus and Saturn. The willfulness of Moon in Aquarius was thus intensified by the square to Uranus. Uranus at Venus/Saturn therefore had to lead to sudden separation (CSI). Venus in the sign of Scorpio is indicative of a passionate nature, which the old man was unable to satisfy.

A woman born July 30, 1882 married at the age of twenty, gave birth to two girls and a boy, but only one girl survived. The twenty-year marriage ended in divorce because of unfaithfulness. This woman's Moon in Aquarius was in exact opposition to Sun in Leo; Uranus, Venus and Mars were located in a very close conjunction in the sign of Virgo, making for a very sexually-oriented disposition, in turn making it difficult for the woman to remain faithful. Already four years after the divorce, the woman had engaged in a liaison with an old man, took care of him up until his death and inherited 40,000 marks, demonstrating her ability to combine her erotic urges with very egoistic and practical ends. Saturn and Neptune were located in Taurus, the sign of "security for life," trine to Venus, Mars, Uranus. An additional configuration also played a significant role: Jupiter 22° Gemini, Uranus 16° Virgo, Mars 18° Virgo, i.e. Mars semisquare to the axis Jupiter/Uranus, which the CSI interprets as follows: "A quick determination, the desire to realize one's ideas at once, love of freedom, the desire to make one's fortune in life, speculations." Her fortune was made through love, for Venus at 16° Virgo in conjunction with Mars.

It has been repeatedly substantiated that a position of Moon in Aquarius frequently leads to relationships between individuals greatly apart in age. There were often several relationships at the same time or in succession which had a great influence on later life. The sign of Aquarius as the eleventh sign is said to correspond to the eleventh house, which relates to friendship. And friendships are often of greater import in life than marriage itself.

If the Moon in the sign of Aquarius very often suggests an unusual love-life, as the cases under discussion have shown, then there are surely very many happy marriages involving this lunar position, so long as the right partner has been found and the relationship is based on genuine love and affection.

Moon in Pisces indicates a very kindhearted, compliant and obliging nature, making it possible for these individuals to adjust to practically any situation. Frequently, these individuals feel misunderstood, are unstable to a certain degree, subject to fluctuations in mood, let themselves drift with the tide, and are not always able to assert themselves, and this can develop into feelings of inferiority. Especially the women feel isolated or become compelled by fate to maintain their reserve or to loneliness.

A woman with Moon in the sign of Pisces suffered very much from her loneliness, because the husband was constantly away on business trips; another woman was condemned to lead a platonic marriage because of the many abdominal operations she had to undergo; yet another was unable to reconcile herself to her fiancé's death and entered no new relationship.

Under a poor aspect of the Moon, there is the inclination to indulge in stimulants and the like (alcohol), unstableness and seductibility. Secret relationships are rather enjoyed.

A very happy marriage was led by a woman born August 19, 1875, and her husband, born February 11, 1874. Although the woman had Moon square to Mars, Moon was also at the midpoint of Sun/ Jupiter, from which we may conclude that her marriage was happy.

The Ascendant in the Signs of the Zodiac

The Ascendant in the natal chart is primarily related to character and its relationship to the environment, and as such is of special significance for the marital disposition. After all, the point of the zodiac ascending at the moment of birth is symbolic of the child's separation from the womb, the moment when he commences breathing on his own, and the entire organism becomes independent. At this moment, not only is the child brought into his place in the environment, but also the environment as well as the entire radiation of the cosmos and the earth gain their first influence over this newborn creature. We may therefore presume that this moment is decisive for the individual's physical constitution, appearance, and character. Trained cosmobiologists can therefore often infer from character and appearance the involvement of the Ascendant. Dr. Schwab has carried out a number of experiments in this regard and has achieved a positive score of 73 percent.

However, it must also be taken into consideration that a "strong" celestial body in the vicinity of the Ascendant can gain just as powerful an influence and is capable of bringing about changes in external characteristics. It does indeed make a great difference whether or not Jupiter or Mars or Saturn, for instance, are in the vicinity of the rising point at the time of birth. For this reason, one should not assess the Ascendant on its own, but only in connection with the entire natal chart; it is imperative never to implement the following interpretations by themselves.

Aries at the Ascendant is indicative of a slim, muscular stature, sharp features, a strong-willed character. These individuals are used to pursuing their goals with great zeal and will do the utmost to win the person they judge to be the best partner for them. They are often capable of strong passion and exert themselves to the utmost to bring the partner under their influence, to possess and dominate him. The partners of such persons should therefore never give themselves over completely, but keep something of themselves in reserve in order to give the Arian nature the repeated opportunity to make this "conquest" and thus prevent him from looking for conquests elsewhere, once he has attained his end. Many Arian types also use their unusual energy for some special accomplishment in their profession, whereby their partners may feel neglected.

Taurus on the Ascendant usually shapes individuals of middle stature, who on growing older are prone to stoutness and to disorders of the abdominal organs (Scorpio as the opposite sign). Passion generally has to be kindled. There are personalities among these who desire to be "conquered" and who are by no means as serene inwardly as they may appear on the outside. These individuals never do things in haste and always have concrete and practical ends in mind, they will not marry before their financial basis is secure. Their will tends more to the passive and is expressed more in persistence and obstinacy. These persons do not bow down to force, but demand love, kindness and understanding. Many conflicts arise because of selfish aims. They enjoy indulging themselves in the good and pleasant things life has to offer, they love a cosy, attractive and functional home, yet are inclined occasionally to melancholy. Unfavorable aspects to Mars at the Ascendant, as experience has shown, have brought marriages into danger many a time.

Gemini on the Ascendant indicates a slim and agile physique, the face is full of expression, and when the mouth talks, the hands generally make accompanying gestures. Moods can vary quickly, suggesting great impressionability and somewhat of a nervous disposition. This disposition can sometimes cause conflicts when the partner is unable to show the right kind of understanding or give the proper support, or when he is not willing to act compensatingly in moments of exaltation or of sudden sadness. Gemini types may marry several times if other corresponding factors are present in the natal chart.

Cancer on the Ascendant generally makes for average height, a round face and large eyes. Other characteristics are a reserved or even shy nature, a depth of feeling, sensitivity and perception, domesticity, industry and tidiness. Especially pronounced is the influence of the environment on their moods. These individuals are very affectionate and long for love. They know how to get what they want without any fuss—even if they have to take the roundabout way. They have a very sympathetic heart, like to take care of others and are capable of great sacrifice. If the Ascendant in Cancer is poorly aspected or other bodies are likewise to be found in Cancer or in Capricorn, a tendency for stomach trouble is possible which could be connected to hypersensitivity or moodiness. In good marriages, a large number of children is usually to be expected. The partner of the Cancerian susceptible to moods should have a firmer character and yet be able to go along with the other's emotional trends. Mental and emotional isolation should be avoided at all costs.

Leo on the Ascendant applies to individuals of medium-tall to tall stature (athletic), who appear very self-assured and have a positive attitude towards life, enabling them to overcome crises and difficulties in life more easily. Vitality and love of life can even make a rather negatively-minded partner more enthusiastic. These individuals are keen on playing the dominant role in the marriage and require accommodation of their partners. Tact and kindness will win friends readily, often, with a great deal of skillful maneuvering, little insincerities will be covered up. This generous disposition will also demand of the partner tolerance of some discrepancies. With some there is the propensity for amatory escapades, when other factors in the natal chart also give some indication of this. Individuals with the sign of Leo on the Ascendant can be frequently won over by granting them recognition and meeting their feeling of importance halfway.

Virgo on the Ascendant usually relates to a tall, well-proportioned body, which is well cared for. A certain susceptibility to digestive trouble makes these individuals pay close attention to a natural diet. Their way of living is simple, their nature modest and natural. These individuals are content when life goes along normally and in the accustomed way, but any unforeseen events will influence their mood, and they react with irritation and indecisiveness. They tend to criticize others or even nag. They are very hard to please, and this can result in ill-feeling in the marriage, and yet they themselves are not without faults or foibles, but would like to give the impression that they are infallible.

Libra on the Ascendant as a rule shapes a harmonious and well-built body, which exercises a strong attraction on the opposite sex. These individuals are very congenial because of their friendliness and affability. They like to lean on others and can only develop their capabilities to the full in conjunction with others, and they feel at ease in stimulating company. Individuals under the Libran influence cannot be alone for any long while and should never chose a partner from whom they would be separated for any period of time, e.g. for business reasons, to eliminate the danger of some third person intervening in the marriage.

Scorpio on the Ascendant corresponds mostly to fairly tall and not always well-proportioned individuals with well-cut features and a keen glance. These individuals are fighting natures, are accustomed to getting their way, would like to impose their will on others, but, with a good disposition, are exemplary in their activity and industry. They feel attracted especially to such partners who accommodate themselves to them and do not contradict, otherwise they become irritated or even hot-tempered and brutal. They feel able to cope with all of life's difficulties, are untiring, and can be good partners for individuals of unstable or negative character. Only their own impulsiveness and passionateness has to be kept within bounds, especially when the influence of the ascendant sign is intensified by other bodies as well.

Sagittarius on the Ascendant primarily makes for an agile body, which in younger years is slim, but later on can be inclined to corpulence. These individuals are sociable, can accommodate to a variety of moods, are quick at making close contact, and are also receptive to idealistic ways of thinking. But they also have their own advantage in mind. they love freedom and independence and do not like to take on obligations. Frequently, there will be several love relationships which play a significant role in their lives. Sometimes there will be connections with religious or artistic persons. Partners with firm principles but also great adaptability and versatility will be the best complements.

Capricorn on the Ascendant endows a character with concrete aims, strong will and an untiring capability for work. Such characteristics are necessary, since life seems to have many problems and great tasks in store for these individuals, with the corresponding difficulties to be overcome. Only by strictly concentrating on the essentials and the goal ahead is it possible to assert oneself and achieve success, which usually only comes about in middle age. Capricorn types are usually thin and boney, only later—when they've "made it"—do they put on weight.

These individuals need as their complement someone with a more carefree and cheerful nature, someone who will tear them away from their work and their brooding and apply themselves to the more pleasant sides of life. Fluctuating moods and occasional periods of bad humor could be connected to stomach and digestive trouble.

Aquarius on the Ascendant corresponds mostly to individuals average to tall in size, who are able to win friends easily, who can adapt themselves to others thanks to their sympathy and knowledge of human nature. They usually do things their own way and are very interested in innovations and reforms, and occupy themselves with problems related to the future. They need a partner who on the one hand will provide them with the right kind of understanding, but who on the other hand can at the right time rein in exaggerated zealousness for unrealistic goals and who possesses a good deal of common sense.

Pisces on the Ascendant indicates small to average size persons, who in later years tend to put on weight. An intense inner life, receptivity for all influences, impressionability, reserved nature, and a certain lack of self-assuredness make these individuals seem somewhat negative in their nature, so that they absolutely need a partner who is strong-wilted and has firm principles, in order to influence the Pisces-type positively and help them to assert themselves, and also to prevent their being used by others. These individuals need a partner, too, who in terms of morals can keep them on the right track and can guard them against the bad influence of false friends.

Midheaven (MC) in the Signs of the Zodiac

Midheaven in the natal chart designates the Self, the individual, ego-consciousness, aim in life. Hence there seems to be no justification for this factor not to have been properly taken into consideration up until now in the comparison of cosmograms. Anyone who has delved somewhat deeper into astrology will be aware of the role played by celestial bodies located in the vicinity of the MC, for example, Jupiter or Sun in this area indicate advance in life, or likewise Saturn would make just such an advance very difficult or make for a sharp decline after a peak has been reached. In psychological terms, it depends whether or not the individual has the kind of disposition enabling him, aided by his ego-consciousness, to recognize his aim in life, to assert himself and to achieve recognition, or whether the subconscious functions are stronger, and the individual lets himself drift in a sea of myriad influences, instead of being his own guide and controller of destiny. Pronounced individuality, intensified by the MC, does not fit in well with a personality equally as strong, but rather it is better off with a more adaptable personality. Therefore, if the point of culmination is strongly occupied in both partners' cosmograms, crises are very likely. Harmony is better warranted by an accentuation of the MC in one cosmogram and of the IC in the other. A moderate complementation is achieved when a positive sign in one cosmogram and a negative sign in the other is located at the IC.

Aries at MC reveals a very pronounced goal-consciousness, indicates optimism, ambition and desire to lead, while adaptation or even submission are required for the partner.

Taurus at MC makes for the desire to attain security in life, to pursue all goals with tenacity and perseverance, whereby a certain amount of firm support can be given to a partner less stable in disposition.

Gemini at MC provides the individual with a variety of goals, involving however the danger of a waste of energies, so that a partner should be preferred who possesses greater clarity of vision, as well as concentration and stability.

Cancer at MC endows the individual with a more emotionally accentuated attitude in everything he undertakes, thus being the right complement for a partner who is guided more by reason and practicalities. Yet one's spiritual and emotional attitude can be so pronounced as to render the personality greater in its effect and importance.

Leo at MC indicates the presence of high aims, a constant striving for social advance and self-assertion. In contrast, these individuals require of their partners great adaptability and accommodation, even subordination.

Virgo at MC is indicative of a striving for a stable way of life and financial security. It is also expected of the partner that he likewise adapts himself to this way of life, unless he wants to find himself under constant criticism.

Libra at MC generally makes for great adaptability and harmonious cooperation with the partner, however, this does not exclude the urge to carry out one's own plans and assert oneself.

Scorpio at MC is a significator of ambitious striving, industry and perseverance, as well as acquisitiveness and independence. This energetic nature requires adaptability of his partner, who should also be willing to do his share of the work.

Sagittarius at MC points to a certain degree of open-mindedness toward life, combined, however, with moral probity and a great sense of responsibility, if there are no configurations present to contradict this. These individuals tend to play the leading role in marriage.

Capricorn at MC makes for a show of prudence, patience and perseverance in the individual's leading of his life, whereby he slowly but surely gets his way, and this also provides his partner with a firm stance in life.

Aquarius at MC enables these individuals to grasp at opportunities, recognize new goals and think up new ideas. The partner will receive constant stimulation, but must see to it that goals are pursued energetically and that the aims set are based on more than just Utopian ideas.

Pisces at MC makes for a more wait-and-see attitude, a striving for a quiet life of ease, and so it will depend on the partner to provide the necessary stimulation and expend much of his own energy towards achieving joint success.

Venus in the Signs of the Zodiac

Venus is the planet of love, of mutual attraction as well as of sex life. Venus is connected with the glandular system as a whole and specifically with the sexual organs. Hence if Venus is well-aspected in the cosmogram, sex-life will be harmonious, and if Venus is negatively aligned with other celestial bodies, then sex-life can go awry or there are disturbances in the sexual functions. Since Venus is also responsible for the aesthetic sense, one can read from the Venusian position whether the individual in question possesses a sense of tact and sensitivity with regard to love-life, or whether he is more inclined to an uncontrolled sensuality. The position of Venus in the zodiac is less decisive than its aspects with other celestial bodies.

Venus in Aries is indicative of great passion, which, however, can also be coupled with high ideals about love. At times, love can easily become a form of adolation. The ability to become popular fairly quickly usually remains without any permanent result. If genuinely high ideals are present, they are rarely shared by the partner.

One woman, whose natal chart has Venus in Aries square to Jupiter, was characterized by very high ideals about love, but she only met with misunderstanding and could not assert herself in marriage. Another woman, with Venus conjunction Mercury in Aries, was also imbued with high ideals, very much colored, too, by religious views. In another case, Venus was located in Aries in an opposition to Saturn; this woman talked a lot about the ideal marriage, but separated from her husband for purely material reasons. Venus in Aries conjunction Neptune showed up perverse tendencies. This does not make it out of the question for Venus in Aries to bring about happy relationships as well, with the proviso that Venus is favorably aspected.

Venus in Taurus indicates a strong power of attraction, combined with deep feelings of love and true affection. However, future security and material interests are by no means fully disregarded. These individuals are also capable of fighting to save their marriages. A man, whose cosmogram shows Venus in Taurus in a trine to Moon and Jupiter, was only able to marry the woman he loved after great trials and tribulations, and the marriage remained a happy one. A man who married a woman thirteen years his senior and led a happy married life with her had in his cosmogram Venus in Taurus trine Jupiter. A female chart with Venus at MC trine to Uranus applies to a woman who already married at the age of 17 and who was a valuable helping-hand to her husband in his arts and crafts business. In another case, a woman had Venus located in Taurus in opposition to Uranus, and she had been having an affair for many years, but which did not result in marriage. Venus aspecting Uranus often leads to early or precipitant relationships.

Venus in Gemini makes for a more carefree attitude toward love. There is generally a lot said about ideals, but the energy is lacking to realize them. A partner is needed who can give this kind of "flighty nature" a firm stance. A relationship very often develops on the basis of common interests or working together vocationally. Crises frequently come about due to third persons. Sometimes one's inclinations are divided among several persons, and it is difficult to make a final decision.

A woman whose natal chart had Venus in the sign of Gemini trine Jupiter was a very good housewife and businesswoman; her marriage was at first happy, but did finally end in divorce later because of the presence of other critical aspects. The possibility of being married several times is certainly not rare under Venus in Gemini, especially when Venus is unfavorably aspected. Venus conjunction Neptune led in one case to severe emotional upset, Venus opposition Saturn resulted in separation, and in another case, Venus square Saturn managed to bring about a divorce at an advanced age.

Venus in Cancer is indicative of strong family ties and wealth of feeling, since Venus and the lunar sign combine here, producing especially in a female chart a strong desire for marriage and motherhood. Venus in Cancer is also characteristic for a love which is willing to make sacrifices and which gives more than it receives. Great value is attached to the right kind of home life. The partner is often older, corresponding to the tendency to seek out a man in more mature years or a woman with some experience. If the early urge for motherhood cannot be satisfied by an early marriage, there is danger of an illegitimate union. Very rarely is there a marriage without children under Venus in Cancer. Venus conjunction Jupiter corresponded in one man's case to a short, unhappy union followed up by a very happy marriage and many children.

If unfavorable aspects to Venus appear, separation is often the result, due to the partner's lack of domesticity and his seeking relationships elsewhere. In one case, the husband was a naval officer, and his long absences away from home contributed in part to the subsequent separation, since a woman with Venus in Cancer cannot do without her husband for any length of time. In another case, the husband was a heavy drinker. (Cancer is a water sign!)

Venus in Leo makes for an affectionate and kind heart which finds reciprocation easily enough, but which itself is not always entirely capable of deep feeling or constancy. Latent in the desire for company, pleasures and diversion is the danger that one's heart becomes inflamed with the wrong kind of person. And if the partner tends to be jealous, he would in this case have reason to be. As a rule, however, Venus in Leo allows for a sense of decency, but which can sometimes be stained by unpleasant experiences. Unhappy marriages result under Venus in Leo usually when unfavorably aspected and other configurations point to marital crises. Vanity and self-importance always lead to a desire for good clothes and a luxurious home.

Venus in Virgo allows the mind to play a significant role in matters of love and make for fastidiousness in love, and there is difficulty in making the final decision to marry when impeding configurations are also involved. A lot of thinking and brooding is done about love problems. Disappointments often occur when rational considerations and practicalities take precedence over pure affection. A striving for chastity and moral purity can in the case of a negative positioning of Venus lead to prudery or oddness.

A man with Venus conjunction Mercury and opposition Saturn as well as square Moon in his natal chart avoided all sexual intercourse in his marriage, making his wife ill and hysterical. Many persons with Venus in Virgo at the time of their birth find themselves to be particularly refined in their love technique or have a propensity for perversities, if the corresponding aspects are also involved. Venus in Virgo has frequently been determined to coincide with homosexual tendencies, e.g. Venus square Moon in Gemini (October 8, 1884), Venus opposition Saturn (October 17, 1876), Venus square Neptune (September 27, 1895), Venus square Mars (November 7, 1903).

Venus in Libra, in its home sign, makes these individuals generally very pleasant and attractive to others, and love relationships are taken up fairly quickly, but which are usually only of short duration. They very much enjoy social events and entertainments,,and it is usually at such occasions that they meet their marital partner for the first time. The marriage can be extremely happy as long as the right kind of complementation has been found. It is important in this respect for the partner to be firm in character in order to be able to be the guiding hand in the marriage and keep extravagance down to a minimum. The passionate Venus-Libra nature should be allied to someone who is of a cooler disposition.

With Venus conjunction Mercury, opposition Mars and square Saturn there was a case where the individual was very sensual in nature and could not keep his love of pleasure and enjoyment under control, and as a result he had engaged in a great number of adulterous relationships and amorous scandals. In another case, the marriage was very happy in spite of Venus square Saturn, because other favorable configurations proved to be strong compensating factors.

Venus in Scorpio, which in itself is closely connected to sex, is indicative of a very passionate nature difficult to control. Emotional life is very intense, but this is not always expressed outwardly. The partner is jealously guarded and watched to see if he remains faithful.

When these individuals fall genuinely and deeply in love, they are capable of great sacrifices, can even give up their own identity and fully immerse themselves in the other person. The natal chart of a man with Venus in Scorpio and without any other aspects besides the quadrature to Moon's Node gave evidence of high ideals and unselfishness in marriage. After the death of his first wife, he married a second time, and this marriage, too, was very harmonious.

If Venus in Scorpio is unfavorably aspected by other bodies, marital conflicts and scandal are the likely results. A woman who ran away with another man had in her natal chart Venus opposition Mars with Neptune and square Moon. In another case with a similar constellation, a man's marriage was destroyed by another woman's fanatic love so that she could marry him.

Venus in Sagittarius can easily lead to fanatic love, but can also allow for the development of high ideals. Precipitant unions are usually soon followed up by disillusionment. Hypersensitivity and moodiness can be disruptive to harmony. Since life is often regarded in a somewhat carefree light, it is good when the partner is of very strong character. These individuals may go slightly astray without thinking too much about it. Optimism ought not to lead to imprudence or shallowness.

If Venus is involved in poor aspects, there is then the possibility of being married several times. A man, whose natal chart showed Venus in a square to Mars and Neptune, married a second time at an advanced age, after his wife, with whom he had seven children, divorced him for unfaithfulness. In another case Venus was located in Sagittarius in a conjunction with Mars; the husband filed for divorce because of his affair with his receptionist. A girl who just barely escaped being raped in the very difficult times of 1945 had in her natal chart Venus in Sagittarius square Uranus in Pisces. Another woman also had Venus in Sagittarius, in an exact opposition to Neptune; starting from the sign of Pisces, Mars is located between these two in a square and just out of bounds of the orb for the midpoint Venus/Neptune. This woman is sexually reserved and possesses a great deal of self-control (Sun and Mercury in Sagittarius, Moon/Cancer, Ascendant/Leo), yet she gave birth to five children, leads a normal married life and is very elevated and noble in her attitudes towards morals, love, and marriage. She lives her life accordingly—but her husband has watched over her from childhood with almost pathological jealousy, which now, however, seems to be subsiding on their approaching the thresh-hold of old age. In the cosmogram of a proprietor of a brothel and sex-criminal Venus was in opposition to Neptune. However, there were other configurations present which implied a criminal disposition, and again we see that quick conclusions should never be drawn from one single configuration on its own.

Venus in Capricorn need not mean, as the "Saturnian sign" might lead one to suppose, a cold disposition. Love is usually taken very seriously. Even the slightest disappointment can be a cause for mistrust and jealousy. In many cases, obligation and loyalty will be given precedence over love and relationships maintained, even when they have already cooled down. Often, there is an inclination for a partner considerably older than oneself. Many individuals with this Venus position may be capable of a very deep attachment, but are unable to demonstrate this love without difficulty, because of their aversion to any kind of external show, a result of inward inhibition. These individuals cannot show affection, but they can be faithful. A great number of children is seldom the case with this Venus position. In the cases at hand, only very rarely were more than two children born. Oftentimes, vocational reasons lie at the root of this. Venus in Capricorn has been found many times to be present with women who work.

Aberrations of love are very possible with individuals of low origin, or with some hereditary disease, or who are strongly inhibited. A pastor (December 9, 1899), whose natal chart contained Venus in Capricorn, as well as Saturn and Neptune in opposition at the midpoint of Sun/Venus, was homosexually inclined. And in the case of another homosexually inclined clergyman, Venus was in Capricorn in a square to the midpoint Moon/Saturn (February 6, 1888).

Venus in Aquarius usually relates to a marriage made on the grounds of certain ideals, in some special cases even for the purpose of creating a "superman." There is almost always a very special attitude about love and marriage. If a marriage cannot be kept intact, these individuals are able to go their separate ways without there being any ill-will between them. Altruism often takes the place of individual love. Philosophical and religious questions often play a role. Many individuals with Venus in Aquarius renounce marriage in order to apply themselves entirely to some social work. With these individuals, love seems to seek some spiritual manifestation. To my knowledge, there is only one case under a favorable aspect of Venus where the marriage ended in a divorce. One woman, who had married a man very much in debt, even managed to help him on his way upwards again.

Venus in Pisces makes for depth of feeling and strong affection, but these first have to be stimulated and kindled. With this Venus position, strange destinies in love are often the case, which range from severe inner isolation to an active love of mankind. The longing for love is always great and does not always attain fulfillment. When too trusting these individuals may come under the influence of others, be used, and, finally, suffer disappointment. Bad company should always be avoided in order to make even the slightest wrong step unlikely.

A woman, who had in her natal chart Venus in Pisces in conjunction with Sun and square to Uranus and Saturn, was sexually molested, had a number of miscarriages and was in many hospitals and sanatoriums (Pisces, the sign of isolation, of locked up buildings!). A man, whose cosmogram had Venus in Pisces in opposition to Mars, had a number of secret liaisons. Venus square Saturn was contained in the natal chart of a man whose wife drowned (Pisces = a water sign!). A woman who was living with a man for quite a while had in her chart Venus in

Pisces without any exceptional aspects.

If Venus is well-aspected and there are no other signs indicating a bad marriage, a very good relationship to the partner can exist under Venus in Pisces. This was one man's experience, who had Venus trine Moon in his natal chart. A woman with Sun conjunction Venus in her cosmogram not only led a harmonious married life but also devoted herself to philanthropies, and thus fully corresponds to her cosmic disposition.

Mars in the Signs of the Zodiac

Mars is the planet of willpower as well as of procreative power and sex. Therefore, Mars will inform us as to what extent one's own will gains influence over that of the partner or vice versa to what extent one's own volition becomes subject to the partner's, as well as the degree to which the power of resistance or tractability. the desire to lead or adaptability are present. Again, it must be taken into consideration that the position of Mars in the zodiac is not atone the deciding factor, but that the aspects to the other celestial bodies play an equally significant role. Mars trine Jupiter corresponds to a harmonious will. Mars square Saturn or Uranus leads to violent actions. Mars in favorable aspects to Venus makes for a harmonious sex-life, whereas poor aspects to Venus can easily result in excess or an abnormal disposition.

Mars in Aries indicates a very strong will which demands subordination on the side of the partner. All goals are pursued with indefatigable energy, so that there is nothing for the partner but to go along in step to order to avoid conflicts. This impulsive nature should meet with understanding and diplomacy on the side of the partner. Love life is conducted along the lines of these individuals' desires. Sexual urge is at times very strong, but can cool down just as readily if the individual himself is too much occupied with other matters. Often, a marriage is entered not for reasons of love but to realize some other intentions. A man, whose natal chart showed Mars trine Saturn, married a woman thirteen years older than himself, because he believed she would useful to his aims. A young woman asserted her will and married a man eighteen years her senior, but was very much disappointed by him, viz. Mars was square Neptune in the cosmogram. A man with Mars conjunction Venus in Aries had an overly active sex-urge, was married and divorced twice.

Mars in Taurus does not make for an impulsive will as in the case of Aries, instead one finds here more steadiness, inflexibility, self-will and obstinacy. Goals are pursued with perseverance and patience, and a striving for material gain plays a great role as well. This Mars position is frequently to be found with entrepreneurs (business), who because of their energy and practical know-how are able to make their way. Women with Mars in Taurus can be very practically-minded housewives. Since Scorpio is the opposite sign of Taurus, and Taurus is also "ruled" by Venus, the sexual drive is usually fairly strong, and there are often illnesses in connection with the sexual organs. A young man with Mars in Taurus in opposition to Moon and Uranus suffered from onanism. Women are very prone to abdominal trouble when Mars is unfavorably aspected. Frequently, strong hemorrhages will periodically occur. Caution should be taken with operations involving certain organs. A child who had to undergo a genital operation very nearly bled to death.

Since Mars in Taurus is often indicative of a biased or dogmatic outlook on things, there should be no great difference in religion if a marriage is planned in order to eliminate all conflicts in this sphere.

Mars in Gemini points to good adaptability and flexibility, so that it is all to the good if the partner possesses great energy. Since will is manifested more intellectually than emotional-la, there is usually the propensity for hasty criticism, provocation, and perhaps even quarrelsomeness. Therefore, it is advisable for the partner to be rather "thick-skinned," making him less likely to be provoked. Likewise the tendency toward dissipation of energies or superficiality has to be checked by the partner, as it is possible for these individuals not to take love or faithfulness too seriously. There are some examples with Mars in Gemini trine Moon and Mars trine Sun corresponding to very liberal views on love. Mars in Gemini makes it of special significance as to how the partner cosmograms relate to one another, whether there are any compensatory aspects present, for example through Jupiter or whether critical aspects to Saturn or Uranus can be determined.

Mars in Cancer can make will dependent on emotion. Fluctuations in mood are very frequent and can easily lead to disharmony. Poor aspects often result in domestic strife. There is nonetheless the endeavor to keep the marriage intact, even when there are enormous differences of opinion, and especially when children are involved. Mars often dictates in the "lunar sign" Cancer instinctive action motivated by unconscious impulse for which there is no rational explanation. Women with Mars in Cancer are almost always very domestic and very much concerned with the family's well-being. If a marriage does break up, it is seldom the fault of the partner whose natal chart contains Mars in Cancer. A woman with Mars in Cancer had a difficult struggle to win the love of a certain man, but she prevailed. In another case. Mars was located in conjunction with Moon and in a square to Saturn, and yet the marriage was harmonious, the only dark side was the husband's nervous condition. A man whose cosmogram even had Mars square to Uranus says his marriage is a very happy one.

Mars in Leo endows the individual with a strong will and accordingly the right to be the leading partner in the marriage.

However, generosity in every respect makes a harmonious marriage possible, although some modicum of adaptation is required of the other partner. Under good aspects of Mars a strong sense of responsibility is usually present and the confidence of others is rarely disappointed. The heart (Leo) is a motivator in all actions, however, this is not only for the sake of the family, but for others as well, a tendency which may be misunderstood by the partner. Bad aspects of Mars in Leo can allow love of power or uncontrolled passion to become manifest in a lapse in morals. In general, one can say that individuals with Mars in Leo demand much of others but also give a lot.

Mars in Virgo corresponds to a conscious directing of energies, concentration on details and a critical attitude, without the involvement of too much feeling. A goal is always based on what is practical and useful, decisions are made difficult by an overly keen critical sense. These points find in part their application in love life and marriage as well. Here, too, very pragmatic considerations are made in connection with marriage, and sensitive and more emotionally oriented persons may suffer under this kind of attitude as they may feel neglected. Strong vocational demands on these individuals mean they tend to be nervous and irritable at home. (This sensitivity and irritability can also be due to digestive trouble.) The vocation may also require occasional separations from home. A man who led a very happy married life had to go on frequent trips abroad, and he had Mars in Virgo trine Moon. In another case. Mars was located in conjunction with Venus; this couple had many children, but the man was very often away from the family for business reasons.

Mars in Libra is related to a strong desire for love and enables these individuals to win the hearts of others easily, although the dictates of faithfulness are not always upheld. However, there are several cases known where genuine affection prevailed, in so far as the right partner had been found. A man whose natal chart had Mars in Libra called his marriage with an artist very harmonious. The Mars position is especially good for vocational collaboration. However, there is danger in a situation where this collaboration is with woman, while the wife stays at home, or vice versa, when the wife in her job has a lot to do with men. A woman whose cosmogram had Mars in Libra square to Sun made a conquest of her married boss, needless to say the marriage did suffer from it. It is in any case advisable for individuals with Mars in Libra not to indulge in any "experiments" with regard to love.

Mars in Scorpio indicates not only great energy and activity directed toward some goal but also a strong sexual urge. The "indestructability" of these individuals requires a great deal of adaptation of their partners. The partner who best suits these individuals is of good health and able to produce children. Just as in the case of Mars in Taurus there is also the danger here of abdominal trouble. It is of advantage if vocation makes great demands on energy or in someway fits in with the Martian nature. For instance, this Mars position was ascertained in the cosmogram of a midwife, who herself remained single, but who was of aid to a great number of women in delivering their children. When Mars is poorly aspected and there are no good correlations to the partners' cosmogram, violence and conflicts may be the result.

Mars in Sagittarius makes the individual enthusiastic about the ideal marriage, but does not imbue him with sufficient energy to realize on his own the goals involved. It is therefore necessary for him to have a partner possessing greater steadfastness and firmness. Sometimes marriages are entered into without proper consideration beforehand and just as soon end in divorce. Being married several times, and not necessarily unhappily, is also frequently the case. No marriage at all is very rare under this Mars position.

Mars in Capricorn makes for a strong, persistent and tenacious will, so that the partner should be adaptable and pliant, or even diplomatic, in order to guarantee continued harmony. A great deal of self-control can be called upon with regard to sex life, but these natures can by no means be considered to be as cold as they might appear. However, there will be times when the partner feels neglected or at a disadvantage because of the demands placed on the other by profession or some special endeavor, and the partner is thought of more as a comrade or colleague than as a member of the opposite sex. Women with this Mars position do not want only to play the role of the housewife, they also want to participate in the husband's activities, if not actively then at least passively. If there is no correspondence of goals between the partners or alienation begins to develop, a quick decision is then imperative.

Mars in Aquarius is productive of more goals and wishes than can be realized. The desire for new stimulations, change and diversion requires that the partner's aims can be adjusted accordingly. Matrimonial unions are made more in the sense of a comradeship or working partnership, so that a certain amount of freedom is left to both partners. Old habits and conventionalities are left by the wayside because there is the desire to do things in one's own way.

A harmonious marriage can evolve under good aspects of Mars. This was one woman's case whose natal chart had Mars trine to Jupiter. In many cases, the marriage may have been all that it should have been, but the individuals involved suffered because they could not attain other goals they had set themselves. A woman with Mars square Venus and Neptune admitted she had found satisfaction neither as a human being, nor a woman nor as an artist, for which the unfavorable Neptune position must have been largely responsible. One woman whose cosmogram contained Mars in Aquarius in an opposition to Uranus married a foreigner, did a lot of traveling, but did not remain faithful, because her eccentric desires could not be satisfied in her marriage.

Mars in Pisces allows for no great willpower, and this negative sign makes for the expenditure of energy often without any noticeable effect. The adaptability of these individuals requires a stronger will in the partner. There is often a tendency to solitude, also to secret association. A man whose natal chart had Mars in a trine to Moon was very happily married; however, his wife died very young, and he never remarried. A woman whose cosmogram contained Mars in an opposition to Moon and square to Sun had an affair with a married man for many years, but she broke it off and got married at the age of 34. There are many cases where individuals with Mars in Pisces have to suffer being beaten or otherwise mistreated by their partners.

Jupiter, Saturn, Uranus, Neptune, Pluto and the Moon's Node in the Signs of the Zodiac

Jupiter to Pluto and the Moon's Node do not relate so much to the individual as to an age group or whole generations. This is due to the length of each planet's stay in a particular sign: Jupiter on the average of one year, Saturn more than two years, Uranus seven years, Neptune fifteen years, and Pluto almost thirty years. Therefore, more depends in these cases on the mutual aspects than on the position in the individual signs.

Jupiter is not only the planet of happiness, but also of harmony, law and religion. According to older text-books, Jupiter is also the planet of the legitimate marriage. It does, however, seem to be a rather vain endeavor to try and see from favorable or unfavorable Jupiter aspects just how legitimate a marriage is, one might as well try to read from the natal chart whether the child was born out of wedlock or not.

Saturn is the planet of inhibition and separation. Therefore it indicates in individual natal charts whether a person has to overcome inner restraints, or cannot make contacts easily, or whether a lack of adaptability may lead to separation, or whether the individual has been endowed with the ability to associate with others easily and openly.

Uranus is said to be the planet of suddenness, of overriding change, transformation and rhythm. If it is prominently aspected in the natal chart, then many sudden changes in life are in store for the individual; if the normal course of life is disrupted, changes in character, in the outlook on life and in the way of life are the result. Even marriage can mean a complete change in life, likewise the breaking up of a marriage.

Neptune is primarily related to the unconscious forces in man, his receptivity, impressionability and imagination. Good aspects will influence the individual in a positive sense, he has clear-cut ideas, desires and plans. Unfavorable planetary configurations will result in a lack of clarity, in confusion, peculiar ideas and inclinations.

In the four decades since its discovery **Pluto** has as yet remained a fairly unknown planet to us. However, we may presume that it has special application to community spirit, and that its position in the natal chart often involves an unusual relationship of the individual to others, and that in this the experiences shared by whole generations play a great role, likewise, too, experiences which are beyond the control of the individual. These mass experiences include for example the World Wars, mass emigrations and resettlements and their consequences. Of course, very much depends on how the individual himself reacts in such periods and on the extent to which he lets himself be influenced and changed in his thinking and actions.

The **Moon's Nodes**, which represent the intersection of the solar and lunar orbits, is also of great significance in human life with regard to the relationships among individuals, on the one hand with regard to the individual's blood relations, and on the other with regard to his marital relationship. A favorable configuration of the ascending Node (Dragon's Head—the descending Node, Dragon's Tail, is always located directly opposite in the zodiac) pertains to adaptability, companionship, and a desire for association; an unfavorable aspect results in a lack of adaptability and difficulties in relations, or even separation.

III

Significant Aspects for Love and Marriage

In our discussion frequent mention has been made of the fact that the position of the celestial bodies in the zodiac is not the sole deciding factor, but rather, their mutual aspects are of crucial significance. Of course, all aspects can be related in some way or other to love and marriage, but there are some which in particular play a predominant role.

Sun and Moon are the incorporation of man and woman. When forming a trine or sextile to one another, and no harmful aspects to other bodies are present, they are favorable influences on the relationship between husband and wife. In the case of oppositions, inner tensions are possible coupled with the inclination for occasional irritability, which, however, does not necessarily mean that love-life itself suffers. Likewise squares between Sun and Moon do not have to be as critical in effect as they are often represented to be. However, in such cases Mars and Venus should at least be favorably aspected.

Sun and Venus are of significance for physical love. Conjunctions, sextiles, and trines can be regarded as especially favorable, but even semisquares, squares, and oppositions promote physical attraction, although marital crises are very likely when Saturn, Uranus, Neptune or Pluto touch the squares as transits or directions.

Sun and Mars produce the power of assertion in all aspects. Under harmonious aspects, the individual is prone to be the boss in marriage and is acknowledged in this function. With conjunctions, squares, oppositions there is always the danger of conflicts and disputes arising from too strong an urge for power.

Sun and Jupiter bring about not only recognition and success under favorable aspects but also good health and those moral qualities which are absolutely essential to a harmonious marriage. Present in a female natal chart, this can mean social advance through marriage. Squares and oppositions are not exactly unfavorable, but they do signify increased demands and unnecessary expenditure.

Sun and Saturn in a harmonious aspect (sextile, trine) make for steadiness, perseverance, constancy. Conjunctions, squares, and oppositions usually suggest inhibitions which make getting better acquainted with others rather difficult and which can lay the groundwork for alienation and separation. One's health is in some respect weakened. Difficulties with the husband are indicated in the female cosmogram.

Sun and Uranus in sextile or trine suggest a personality full of originality, which always has a very stimulating effect on the environment. Conjunctions, squares, oppositions, however, indicate obstinacy, impatience, contradictory behavior and often given rise to mutual upset.

Sun and Neptune in favorable aspects signify good powers of imagination, idealism and enthusiasm. We may conclude from conjunctions, squares, and oppositions weakened health on the one hand, and on the other, the danger of disappointments due to false conceptions. An unfavorable position in the female chart may indicate disappointment because of the husband.

Sun and Pluto in favorable aspect point to the power of assertion and leadership ability and desire. Critical aspects in female charts often resulted in separation through force majeure, e.g. separation or premature death due to war, mishap, arrest, etc.

Sun and Moon's Node are related to spiritual, physical or family relationships.

Sun and Ascendant indicate, according to aspect, a harmonious or disharmonious attitude towards others.

Sun and MC relate to personal relationships which are also connected with one's aim in life.

Moon and Venus are the heavenly bodies of love and devotion, so that harmonious aspects here would indicate a deep and loving relationship, while critical positions of these two factors can mean moodiness, irritability, conflict.

Moon and Mars are significators of an emotionally-directed will, especially of the unconsciously motivated actions, and perhaps also the instinctual liking for another person. If Moon and Mars are located unfavorably, there is a proneness for impulsiveness, increase of unmotivated emotional excitability, which in turn can lead to disharmony and strife. Favorable aspects are indicative of a harmonious relationship of the man to the woman, unfavorable aspects frequently lead to upset and conflict.

Moon and Jupiter when favorable point to popularity, the happy (Jupiter) woman (Moon), or also to the woman who brings happiness, whereas critical aspects suggest indifference, negligence, and extravagance. There is difficulty in making proper use of money, and this results in conflicts.

Moon and Saturn in unfavorable aspects lead to inhibitions, lack of adaptability, difficulty in making contact with others, troubled relationship to mother or wife, and can also mean the danger of a separation. In the female natal chart, this can also be connected with physical ailments.

Moon and Uranus in favorable aspects are stimulating in their effect, in unfavorable aspects they lead to great inner tension, to a propensity for upset and unpremeditated acts, self-will, and stubbornness.

Moon and Neptune in sextile or trine indicate great sensitivity, in conjunction, square, and opposition false or misguided sentiments, illusions, self-deception, instability or even mendacity, so that these weaknesses of character can easily result in the disturbance of a relationship.

Moon and Pluto are likely to lead to an one-sided intensification of feeling and in favorable terms to a refined sensitivity and a psychometric talent, and in unfavorable terms they can result in periodic emotional outbreaks, whereby the motivation is always the same, be it jealousy, offended vanity, etc.

Moon and Moon's Node are connected with emotionally accentuated relationships and spiritual contact.

Moon and Ascendant refer to the personal relationship to other persons, to women in particular.

Moon and MC in conjunction, sextile, trine indicate a deep nature and rich emotional life, whereas squares suggest slightly changing attitudes, and oppositions can influence the personal aim in life via the unconscious.

Mercury and Venus in harmonious aspects promote the ability to establish contact and the development of love (Venus) thoughts (Mercury).

Mercury and Moon's Node in harmonious aspects foster mutual interest and exchange of ideas.

Venus and Mars deserve special attention with regard to love and marriage, since they represent the love (Venus) impulse (Mars), mutual attraction, liking and, finally, the physical union for the purpose of procreation. If Venus and Mars form no aspects or midpoints at all, this can be interpreted as a lack of sexual urge or disturbances in this report. An unfavorable aspect is always better than none at all. A conjunction designates a very strongly sensual nature, which often lacks delicacy of feeling and tact. Square and opposition imply a pronounced sexuality bringing with it the danger of periodic exaggeration or aberration. Sextile and trine make for a harmonious expression of sexuality and also indicate creativity in some art form.

When Venus and Mars are positioned favorably, but Sun and Moon are unfavorable, sexual unions are possible, but which are only temporary in nature.

Venus and Jupiter are the factors applying to love's (Venus) happiness (Jupiter). Those individuals having these two bodies in their natal chart in harmonious aspect are capable of easy contact with members of the opposite sex, of making themselves liked, and will be happily married, as long as there are no other powerful configurations to the contrary. Venus in a square or opposition to Jupiter by no means diminishes the power of attraction, but it does make improper behavior and lack of constancy in love relations possible.

Venus and Saturn in favorable aspect indicate constant love and fidelity, but in conjunction, square or opposition point to love suffering, difficulty in relating to others, or a temporary alienation. Simultaneous involvement in critical aspects with other celestial bodies (Uranus, Neptune, Pluto, Mars) makes infidelity (even prostitution), renunciation, loneliness, and in some cases childlessness likely. The causes for this can be found in poor health, impediment of the inner secretions, etc., especially when Taurus and, Scorpio are heavily occupied.

Venus and Uranus in mutual aspect point to feelings of love which develop suddenly, "love at first sight," but which rarely result in permanent relationships. These individuals can become quickly enamored, are even capable of engaging in some amorous escapade all on the sudden, but which just as quickly comes to an end. The critical effect is possible especially through conjunction, square, and opposition.

Venus and Neptune in favorable aspects imply ideal love or even rapture and, in the case of conjunction, square, opposition, lack of good taste, instability, false feelings of love, jealousy, aberration or disappointment in love.

Venus and Pluto point to intensified feelings of love, and in conjunction, square or opposition, to emotional extremes.

Venus and Moon's Node in good aspects make for adaptation, obligingness, sincerity.

Venus and Ascendant in favorable aspects are significators of a harmonious attitude towards the opposite sex.

Venus and MC imply a deeply-felt personal love when located in a conjunction, sextile or trine.

Mars and Jupiter in a good aspect typify not only successful (Jupiter) activity (Mars) but also fortuitous decisions and a happy marriage coupled with the urge to be the dominant partner. At the time of marriage itself (as well as births) transits or directions of Mars and Jupiter are usually due. When Mars and Jupiter form a square or opposition, they also promote the decision to marry, however, in many cases differences in the outlook on life or religion have often been ascertained.

Mars and Neptune in unfavorable aspects may mean abuse or weakening of sexuality, and in Scorpio the danger of infection, venereal disease.

Mars and Moon's Node in good aspects foster the urge (Mars) to unite, to get married (Moon's Node), while unfavorable aspects may disrupt matrimonial life.

Jupiter and Saturn in unfavorable aspect signify an impediment to marriage or marital difficulties, in which differences in outlook may play a role, and in favorable aspects they imply perseverance, patience, sense of duty.

Jupiter and Uranus in favorable aspects mean good luck in life, and this may include a love union which has come about suddenly. Jupiter in a square or opposition to Uranus may lead to sudden turns, tensions or even a sudden dissolution of a union.

Jupiter and Moon's Node may, in harmonious aspects, result in good relationships, pleasant associations, and also a happy marriage.

Jupiter and Ascendant in conjunction, sextile or trine make for a harmonious personality, who is very congenial and can play the dominant role in society as well as in the family in an agreeable manner.

Jupiter and MC in mutual aspect enable the individual to be dominant not only in his vocation but also in the family without disrupting harmony.

Saturn and Moon's Node in conjunction or square result in a lack of adaptation, as well as to inhibitions as regards relations with others, and the danger of alienation and separation.

Saturn and Ascendant in conjunction, square, opposition make relating to others difficult and can easily lead to alienation and separation.

Saturn and MC in conjunction, square, opposition are indicative of individuals who have many inhibitions and external difficulties to cope with, so that they need a partner who can bring happiness and is positive in nature.

Uranus and Moon's Node in aspect indicate sudden experiences in communal life.

Uranus and Ascendant in conjunction, square or opposition point to a great deal of disturbance in the environment and in the family. Such individuals upset not only themselves, but others as well.

Neptune and Moon's Node in conjunction, square, or opposition may undermine relationships through lack of fellowship or through peculiar behavior (gossip, slander).

Neptune and Ascendant in conjunction, square, opposition lay bare a lack of resistance and can easily lead to disappointment.

The aspects not listed here have little reference to love and marriage and the CSI can be consulted to check up on them.

With regard to the correct assessment of the aspects reference should be made here to Parm's figurative method, which bases its differentiation between harmonious, conjunctional, and oppositional cosmograms on the distribution of the heavenly bodies in the natal chart. Accordingly, to take one example, oppositions are favorable in effect in harmonious horoscopes, unfavorable in conjunctional, and weak in polar horoscopes.[11]

IV

Celestial Bodies in the House of Marriage

Astrological tradition divides the natal chart into twelve sectors or houses. The point of culmination or Midheaven (MC = medium coeli) is always the beginning of the tenth house and the Ascendant the beginning of the first house. Since there are several house systems. each with their solid block of adherents, we shall be concentrating in the present discussion primarily on the corners of the cosmogram, i.e. the points of intersection of the horizon. Ascendant and Descendant, and those of the meridian, the medium coeli and the imum coeli. The area around the Descendant is termed the seventh or marriage house. Experience has shown that the Ascendant mainly pertains to the immediate environment, which helps to shape the personality; the horizon represents more or less the level of experience; and the Descendant shows up the relationships to others, to the individual's alter ego. Thou, and to the public at broad. The Descendant can therefore in general terms be called that area in the cosmogram which represents the individual's attitude to others as a whole and to the marital partner in particular. The 7th house should, however, not be strictly delineated according to the tables of houses, but rather close attention should be paid to the interpretive factors located directly above or below the Descendant. The absence of any factors in this vicinity should by no means lead to the conclusion that the individual concerned either will marry or is not destined to do so, instead, his marital disposition and family life are to be derived from other configurations.

By no means should finished conclusions be drawn from the configurations around the Descendant without due consideration of the entire natal chart and especially the aspects to the other celestial bodies.

You will very often find that the Ascendants in the partners' natal charts lie opposite one another, so that the marriage house of the one partner coincides with the Ascendant of the other, that in a certain respect the individual's personality is merged with that of the other, the Thou, his alter ego. But even when this ideal situation is not the case, you will find several instances where in the one partner's chart the upper half and in the other's chart the lower half, or the east in one partner's chart and the west in the other's is more heavily occupied, corresponding more to an ego-conscious (MC), a subconscious (IC), a positive (Ascendant) or negative (Descendant) attitude towards the partner, respectively, and therein lies the complementation. It is of especial significance if for example the one partner's Sun coincides with the other's Moon in the house of marriage or on the Ascendant, or if one partner has Venus and the other Mars at IC. There are cases where the occupation of the cardinal points or houses play a more significant role than the distribution in the zodiac. In the first example, the woman's chart has Moon, Mercury and Moon's Node close by the MC, the man's has Sun and Venus at this location, and this resulted in a very harmonious union.

Sun on the Descendant promotes the urge to gain public recognition and also to play the dominant rote in the family. Women with this solar position will also seek to attain a broader radius of influence not limited to their own home and family.

Moon on the Descendant is of particular significance in the male cosmogram, where it can give some indication, according to aspect, of the wife's character. All aspects reveal a strong accent on emotion and feeling with more or less fluctuating affection. Favorable aspects indicate a deep and loving relationship (Venus, Jupiter), unfavorable aspects signify disillusionment (coming down to earth) and alienation (Saturn), upset and quarrels (Mars, Uranus), disappointment (Neptune) or emotional and mental shock (Pluto).

Mercury on the Descendant, as tradition has it. pertains to individuals who are prone to make a profit out of marriage or who marry or are married for gain. If the nurtured hopes are not fulfilled. there is imminent danger of separation. Elsbeth Ebertin includes in her book *Astrologie und Liebesleben*[10], the case of a woman, born July 5, 1888, at 6:00 p.m. near Ammersee in Bavaria, whose natal chart had Mercury square Mars. She was in great danger of being poisoned because of another woman. The conjunction between Moon and Neptune is also characteristic. Critical aspects are at least sure to produce much upset and conflict. If there are good aspects to Mercury, mutual interests and vocational teamwork can bring success.

Venus on the Descendant traditionally indicates lovely or rich women in male charts, but this is by no means a guarantee for marital harmony. There has been repeated substantiation of the fact that Venus at this position makes for deep mutual affection and feeling. Good aspects to Venus at this position forge at any rate a very strong bond. Unfavorable aspects, in particular such through Saturn or Neptune, point to abnormal inclinations, aberrations, lack of adaptability in emotional and physical terms.

Mars on the Descendant pertains to the joint struggle for existence or marital conflicts, and, in the case of very critical aspects, to acts of violence. One of the partners will in any event have to be very indulgent and accommodating in order to maintain harmony. Many difficulties may also have their source in the one partner becoming ill, which can represent a threat to financial security. Under good aspects with Jupiter or Venus, there are possibly joint advances in life in store for a harmonious marriage.

Jupiter on the Descendant indicates a complementary nature strongly influenced by Jupiter, suggesting not only a happy marriage but also social advance through marriage, when Jupiter is located "on his own" or is involved in favorable aspects. Critical aspects make marital or public conflicts likely.

Saturn on the Descendant points to inhibitions with others, impedes getting married, brings about worries, sickness or financial trouble coupled with the danger of a subsequent separation, especially under critical aspects. Favorable aspects can alleviate the Saturnian influence and indicate a serious-minded, industrious and conscientious spouse.

Uranus on the Descendant is related to a love of freedom and independence coupled with the striving never to subordinate oneself and always to go one's own way. A lot of adaptability is therefore required of the partner, that is if the right partner is to be found at all. However, there is the possibility that the partner is under the Uranian influence and is the cause of much unrest in the home. Under favorable aspects, the mutual relationship can be very stimulating; boredom will hardly rear its head in such a marriage. Critical aspects can result in a great deal of upset and many dramatic scenes, which subsequently lead to separation. The inclination for amatory adventures and infidelity is very likely.

Neptune on the Descendant in good aspects points to idealistic inclinations and special goals with regard to marital conduct. Under unfavorable aspects, exaggerated wishes will not be fulfilled, great disappointment (possibly through a swindler) and emotional suffering ensue. Oftentimes there is the inclination for peculiar behavior or perversity and other sexual aberrations. Neptune in this position can in the case of very upstanding and moral individuals be conducive to purely platonic relationships. However, more frequent are the cases where no deep spiritual understanding is achieved.

Pluto on the Descendant produces the desire for absolute predominance in the marriage, whereby the attempt is made to put the partner completely under one's thumb. Marriage usually means a complete change in circumstances. Under favorable aspects it is usually easier to find the right, adaptable partner, critical aspects mean the imminent danger of separation, in particular Pluto square or opposition Sun (with women) and Moon (with men). A separation is often brought about through Providence, i.e. through war, mass destiny, arrest, etc.

V

The Midpoints

The midpoints make it possible to discover the fine details of the cosmogram. The word midpoint is given to mean the half or mean sum of two stellar positions in the natal chart. In the example below, Neptune is located in the middle between Venus and Mars without, however, these bodies forming any mutual aspects. In order to precisely calculate this planetary relationship, or the planetary picture, 0° Aries is always used as the starting point. Thus:

Mars = 16° 11' Libra = 196° 11'
Venus = 12°45' Pisces = 342°45'
The sum of Mars + Venus = 538° 56'
The half sum Venus/Mars = 269° 28'= 29° 28' Sagittarius.

Located on the opposite side of the zodiac is the midpoint (half sum) Venus/Mars at 29° 28' Gemini, whereas Neptune is located at 1°06' Cancer. An orb of 3 to 5° is allowed in the case of aspects, but this orb should not amount to more than 3° in the case of midpoints, the usual orb is 1.1/2°. In this example the orb is approximately 1.1/2°. A planetary picture is written as follows:

Venus/Mars = Neptune
  29° 28'   1°06'

In this example, Neptune is also located at the midpoint of Venus/Moon's Node:

Venus/Moon's Node = Neptune
    0°47'   1°06'

Hence even more exactness could be achieved in this example.

The combination of three interpretive factors does make for a fairly specific statement, which is best derived from the CSI[7]. The relevant textbooks[12] should be consulted for the calculation and interpretation of the midpoints.

The natal chart of a woman born February 14, 1903 (Fig. 27) shows the location of Sun in a conjunction with Jupiter in the sign of Aquarius. Venus as the planet of love is not involved in any exact aspects, Saturn is with Mercury on the Ascendant. There are no bodies on the Descendant. It is therefore difficult to formulate an immediate interpretation. However, if we investigate the cosmic condition of the individual interpretive factors also with regard to the midpoints, other precise clues will develop. In order to determine more readily the position of the celestial bodies at midpoints it is best to use the 90° workboard, where the signs of Aries, Cancer, Libra, and Capricorn fall within the first 30°; the signs of Taurus, Leo, Scorpio, Aquarius from 30 to 60°; and Gemini, Virgo, Sagittarius, Pisces from 60

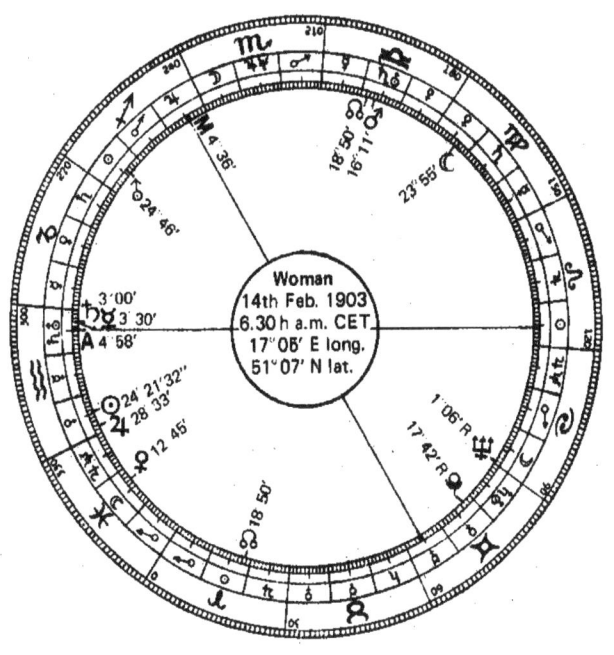

Figure 27

to 90°. The bodies forming conjunctions, squares, and oppositions all cluster together so that a quick survey of the planetary configurations is possible. For instance, Moon and Uranus are next to each other here, although they are square. With the aid of the movable calculating disc, the distance between one body and another is measured, and in this way the midpoints can be easily determined. We differentiate between direct midpoints, as in the case of Neptune above exactly in the middle between Venus and Mars or Venus and Moon's Node, and indirect midpoints, as when a celestial body forms a square, semisquare or sesquiquadrate to the point in question. Sextiles and trines are generally not brought into relation with the midpoints. Saturn, for instance, is located semisquare to Moon/Venus, which is located at 18°20' Sagittarius. Between this point and 3° Aquarius lie 45°, or a semi-square. It is usually advisable first to implement the direct midpoints and consider the indirect midpoints more as supplementary factors.

The CSI is recommended for the interpretation of the midpoints.

We then find the following guidelines:

- Neptune = Venus/Mars: Pathological or abnormal craving in sex-relationship, **the negation of the love-urge**, the inclination to perversity.
- Neptune = Venus/Moon's Node: **Shyness,** feelings of inferiority in love-life. **Reveling or ecstatic love-notions without fulfillment.**
- Mars = Saturn/Neptune: **Weak procreative powers.**
- Pluto = Moon/Venus: Uncontrollable desire for motherhood. (This statement was not realized in fact due to great self-control and—fear of men!)
- Sun = Venus/Saturn: **Unsatisfied desire in love, weak powers of procreation,** a lonely life.
- Sun = Venus/AS: A beautiful body, gracefulness, an appreciation of beauty.
- Saturn = Venus/Uranus: **A controlled sensuality**, suppressed tensions in love-life, **passing sexual and emotional inhibitions.**
- Sun = Neptune/Moon's Node: **Difficulty in establishing contacts with others,** inability to explain one's ideas to others and also the inability to come to an understanding with other people.

Even though Saturn on the Ascendant perforce indicates a nature full of inhibitions, a nature incapable of free and easy contact with others, the midpoints do give a more comprehensive and fairly precise picture.

This is the case of a spinster, "never-been-kissed," and the following was told about her: She is very precise and conscientious in her vocation, industrious, honest and upright. With respect to love, at least, she seems to be afraid of men, she has never had a love affair, and avoided all more personal relations out of a certain sense of propriety. She is healthy and attractive and a man could really get to like her. And now—she is nearly 50—she would perhaps like to get married in order not to be alone in old age. But opportunities are few for her, since she works in a bank and is very much taken up with her job, she also lives fairly secluded and frequents no pleasure spots.

VI

Comparative Analysis Using the 90° Workboard

The aspects do not suffice to uncover all the subtleties involved in the relationship between two partners, and the midpoints do much towards furthering our investigations. In this case, the natal charts are placed on the 90° workboard, and one cosmogram is correlated to the other by setting the calculating disc to point at one of the interpretive factors in the one cosmogram and checking to see at which midpoints of the other chart this factor is located. The following figures present the natal charts of a woman and two men:

1. Female nativity on January 23, 1903, at 11:45 p.m., at 9E52, 48N13.
2. Male nativity on October 14, 1885, at 3:00 a.m., at 8E57, 48N20.

3. Male nativity on January 25, 1892, hour unknown (midday positions).

1. Married October 21, 1934, the wedding itself was postponed until January 2, 1935, due to early commencement of the rainy season in Africa. Marriage very harmonious and happy, daughter born August 17, 1935, husband came down with mysterious disease in November 1937, died August 26, 1938.

2. Married May 28, 1944, 11:00 a.m. in Southern Germany, residence taken up in Czechoslovakia. The husband had seven children out of his first marriage. Son born March 30, 1945, separation in 1946, wife sues for and is granted divorce in 1947.

The female natal chart has alone in the sign of Aquarius five celestial bodies, which is already an indication of peculiarities in the matrimonial circumstances. (Marriage in another part of the world to a man 17 years her senior, taking on seven children.) Sun conjunction Saturn results in inhibitions, retardations, separations. (First marriage delayed because of the rain season, separation through early death, second marriage separated already after two years.) Ascendant conjunction Moon's Node and Mars; trine Pluto, Venus, Mercury and AS at the midpoint Venus/Pluto, according to CSI suggests an attractive personality and unusual love affairs. In addition, Venus is trine to AS, Mars and Pluto and at the midpoint of AS/Pluto. Mercury is located at the midpoint of Venus/Jupiter, and gives rise to hopes of happiness in love. Mars square to the midpoint Saturn/Uranus makes separations possible. Neptune sesquiquadrate to Venus indicates disappointments in the sexual realm (second marriage).

The relationship of the woman to her first husband is characterized by the following mutual aspects:

w:m1 ☉△♇ M.   ♇△☉☿   ♀⚹♂ (M □ ☉ ☿)
      ☉△♅   A♂☿   ☿⚹♂ ♂□♄
      ♄△♀   ☊♂☿☉   ♃□♆ (☽⚹M)
      ♄△♅   ☽△♂   ♀□A (☽□A)
      ♀△☿☉   ♀□♃ ♅□♃☊
      ☿△☿☉   ♆□♅
      ♃△☉☿   ♆⚹☽

The predominance of favorable aspects defines the harmony of the marriage despite the great difference in age, while the unfavorable aspects, especially Mars square Saturn, point to the premature death and the consequent disappointment.

The relationship of the woman to her second husband can be derived from the following mutual aspects:

w:m2 ☉♂☉   ☉□♅
      ☉△♆♀   ☿□☊
      ♆△♀   ♃□☊
      ♆△♅   ♀□♃
      M△♃   ♂□☿
      ☽♂☽?   A□☿
      ♄△♆   ♅□♄
               ♅□♃
               ♅=♃/♄
               ♄♂☉
               ♄□♅

A comparison of the two synastries shows very clearly that in the first union the favorable aspects predominate. We find on taking a closer look at the individual aspects the squares of MC to Sun and Mercury, Moon to AS and Moon opposition M, which need not be regarded as unfavorable, likewise AS square Mercury in the second case. However, in the second case, the Suns and Moons of both cosmograms occupy the same sign of

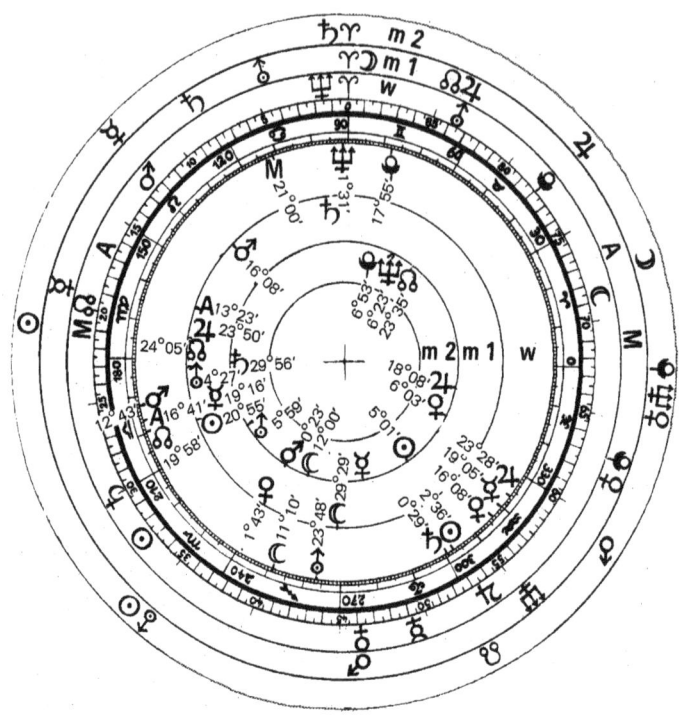

Figure 28
Woman = w = 23 Jan.1903, 11:45p.rn.CET
1st Husband = m 1 = 14 Oct.1885, 3:00 a.m. CET
2nd Husband = m 2 = 25 Jan.1892

the zodiac, indicating not complementation, but similarity of disposition, which generally does not lay the foundation for a harmonious marriage. In the first case, the aspects of the celestial bodies related to love life are very prominent, in particular Venus opposition Mars, Venus trine Mercury, Sun; and Moon trine Mars; in the second case, aspects of Mars and Venus are almost totally lacking, with the exception of Neptune trine Venus. Especially critical aspects in the second case are Uranus square Saturn and Jupiter and Uranus at the midpoint Jupiter/Saturn, and Saturn conjunction Sun and Saturn square Venus. All these aspects indicate separation following a period of great emotional upset.

To achieve a good overall view of the correlations among the three cosmograms. we take a form K 2 with 360° and 90° divisions, draw two additional circles on the inside as well as the outside and enter our positions. We mark each of the cosmograms with w (wife), m 1 (first husband), and m 2 (second husband) respectively.

Of special note in the 360° circle is the location of Sun m 2 in the vicinity of Sun and Saturn w; Sun and Mercury m 1 close by AS and Moon's Node w.

Further aspects are to be readily seen in the 90° circles. Conjoined are Mercury m 1 and Moon's Node w; Mars m 1 and Venus w; Jupiter and Moon's Node m 1 with Uranus w; Jupiter m 2 and Pluto w. We find here that the correlations between w and m 1 are stronger than those between w and m 2.

Of primary interest to us in this investigation are those interpretive factors determining the love and marital relationship, i.e. Sun,

Moon, Venus, Mars, Moon's Node, AS, MC, Jupiter. A consideration of all aspects and midpoints at hand would only incur the danger of too great an accumulation of planetary pictures, which would render a clear-cut overall survey impossible. However, those two do not as yet have much routine in this kind of investigation might still proceed as follows: First the midpoints of each of the cosmograms are ascertained with the aid of the workboard, and then all interpretive factors of the female chart to m 1 and the individual aspects of m 1 to w, and, finally, w to m 2 and m 2 to w at the midpoints are charted.

The procedure can also be such that a survey is made of the most important midpoints of w to m 1 and m 2. We first delineate the relationship between husband and wife in the light of the midpoint Sun/Moon. We therefore adjust the calculating disc to point to the middle of Sun and Moon w. This is, in the 90° circle, at approximately 7° and 52° and, in the 360° circle, at approximately 7° Capricorn. We find on the outside Jupiter w in the vicinity, on the inside, Jupiter is semisquare to Sun/Moon, indicating a felicitous relationship between husband and wife. The CSI is the best aid in working out the interpretation. Saturn m 1 is located at this midpoint, signifying a separation (Saturn) of the marriage (Sun/Moon), in this case through an early death. In addition, we find here Moon's Node m 2 (sesquiquadrate = 135°). indicating the union of man and woman (☊). Characteristically, Moon's Node m 2 is located almost exactly at the midpoint of Sun/Moon m 2. In the case of m 1, Saturn is located at Sun/Jupiter m 1, indicating, among other things, illness. Due to the illness and death of m 1 the marriage (Sun/Moon) of w was destroyed. Saturn m 1 is also located at Venus/Mars m 1, also signifying that the sexual union (Venus/Mars) is disrupted due to Saturn = illness or death.

Sun/Venus designates physical (Sun) love or power of attraction (Venus). In the case of w, this midpoint is located at a tittle over 9° Aquarius. Uranus w is semisquare to this point. M 1 has in the outer circle Jupiter and Moon's Node forming a 135° angle to this point.

The sudden (Uranus) physical love (Sun/Venus) contained in cosmogram w correlates to a happy (Jupiter) relationship (Moon's Node) in m 1's case, and the joint interpretation is: Sudden (Uranus) happy (Jupiter) union (Moon's Node) through physical (Sun) attraction or love (Venus). In the case of m 1, Jupiter with Moon's Node is also located in the 90° circle at the midpoint Uranus/AS, indicating a sudden (Uranus) happy (Jupiter) relationship (Moon's Node) to others (AS). There are no correlating aspects from the side of m 2.

The midpoint Venus/Mars is of special significance for the relationship between the sexes. Mars and Venus in the female cosmogram are trine and form simultaneously a trine to Pluto and AS, whereby Venus is to be found exactly at Pluto/AS. We therefore may presume that w is a strongly sexual nature possessing also a great power of attraction for the opposite sex. However, Neptune w is located in a sesquiquadrate to Venus w, so that the native either leads a somewhat peculiar love life or experiences disappointments in love.

The bond between w and m 1 was definitely the closer one, for Venus w and Mars m 1 coincide in the 90° circle. Moon m 1 but also Saturn m 2 are located opposite along the same axis. In the 360° circle we find Venus w and Mars m 1 in opposition. (As mentioned earlier, an opposition of Venus and Mars in a synastry by no means has to be regarded as unfavorable, in fact this often conduces to a great attraction.) Moon m 1 forms a semisquare to Venus w, Saturn m 2 a sesquiquadrate. The relationship Moon-Venus designates feelings of love, devotion, and, in contrast, Venus-Saturn typifies love suffering.

Venus w is also located at Moon/MC w and Moon/Moon's Node w and means here a personal attachment on the part of the woman. Furthermore, Moon m 1 is at Jupiter/Uranus m 1 and at Uranus/ Moon's Node m 1. This results in a sudden, happy union with a woman. In the case of m 2 with w, Saturn m 2 undermines this personal affection 'and inclination, especially since Saturn m 2 at Uranus/Moon's Node m 2 indicates, according to the CSI, divorce.

The axis Venus/Mars w contains Saturn w as a separating factor affecting the sexual relationship, however, also present is AS m

1 = Venus/Jupiter m 1 and Venus/Moon's Node m 1, characterizing a happy love relationship.

Mars/Venus m 1 does contain Neptune m 1, but also Jupiter w, making for a harmonious sexual relationship between w and m 1.

Venus/Mars m 2 coincides with AS w and Moon's Node w as a designation of the sexual relationship. At the same time, Mars/Neptune m 2 = AS w brings about a disruption of the union, a critical impact is given by Mars/Pluto m 2. Neptune = Venus/Pluto m 2 is characteristic for impressionability, instability, immorality, whereby the woman has to suffer due to MC w at this position, while MC w = Venus/AS and Venus/MC of the first husband makes for deep love and affection.

The following survey correlates the individual midpoints of w with important interpretive factors of m 1 and m 2. For the sake of simplicity, the aspects are symbolized by =.

w	m 1	m 2
☽/☋ = ♆, ♀	= ☽, ♂	= ♄
☽/A = ♀	= ☽	= ♄
☽/M = ♆, ♀	= ☽, ♂	= ♄
♀/♅ = ☋, M	= ☿, ☉	= ♀, ♆, ♀
♀/♀ = A	= ♀	= ♂

The most obvious factor here is the strong position of Saturn m 2 to w, and at this same point we also find in particular Moon and Mars m 1 as correlative factors for the wife.

In order to achieve a comprehensive and thorough evaluation of partner cosmograms it is necessary for AS and MC to be entered as well, on the basis of the birth-time; these points should at least be known in one of the partner's cases. If the hour of birth is unknown, the Moon also has to be deleted because it travels from 12° to 15° in one day, making any exactness impossible.

Of great interest is the comparison of the cosmograms of an 18th century friendship, that of Goethe and Charlotte von Stein. Whereas Goethe himself made his natal chart known, the birth-time in Ch. von Stein's case unfortunately has to be dispensed with, and hence also the points AS and MC. Nonetheless the relationship between the two is very well defined in the configurations.

Prof. H.H. Kritzinger[12] has previously published an explication of the correlations between the two cosmograms and emphasized in particular the mutual conjunction of Sun and Mars in a trine to one another. Goethe's Sun and MC coincide with Charlotte's Sun. Saturn, in the vicinity of Mars in Charlotte's natal chart, is conjunct Goethe's Sun and MC makes clear the self-imposed restraint the two had to undergo. The strength of the bond between Goethe and Ch. von Stein is best seen in the positions of Venus and Jupiter. In Goethe's case Jupiter and Venus are in opposition, and Charlotte's Venus is square to this.

The 90° workboard makes the correlations even more readily discernible. In the female natal chart, we see Venus at the midpoint of Sun/Mercury, and this characterizes the attitude to love-life. This configuration coincides with Venus/Jupiter in the male cosmogram in a semisquare to Sun/Moon's Node and Moon's Node/MC, which according to CSI indicates an interest in the arts, connections with artists and dilettantes, as well as the revelation of feelings and inclinations, and hence this configuration tells us that artistic interests brought these two individuals together, or that this love relationship inspired Goethe in his artistic creativity.

Turning the calculating disc to point at Goethe's Saturn, we find this falls on the axis Venus/Mars and Mars/Jupiter, acting as a restraint on sexual urges (Venus/Mars) and impeding a decision to marry (Mars/Jupiter). Ch. von Stein has at the same location Sun/ Venus semisquare to Pluto, which on the one hand leads to pronounced erotic excitability and on the other to a fateful love affair (cf. CSI). At the same time. Charlotte has Pluto at Saturn/Uranus, signifying "the desire to overcome a difficult situation through extraordinary effort, rebellion against one's lot in life." Let us now turn the calculating disc towards the female Jupiter, this then falls on the axis Venus/Mars, and Goethe's Venus/Saturn in the same position on Sun/Venus, Sun/Jupiter, Venus/MC, Jupiter/MC.

An analysis of these configurations gives us the following picture:

Charlotte von Stein:
- Jupiter = Venus/Mars: healthy sex-life, strong sexual attraction, rich emotional life.
- Jupiter = Venus/Saturn: desire for seclusion, happiness in seclusion, extramarital relationship.

Charlotte von Stein to Goethe:
- Jupiter w = Sun/Venus m: success in love or the arts.
  Jupiter w = Sun/Jupiter m: joint bliss and happiness.
  Jupiter w = Venus/MC m: desire to give love, affection.
- Jupiter w = Jupiter/MC m: achieve success, the value of finding "a noble and fine human soul" (CSI).
- Jupiter w = Mercury/Mars m: constructive criticism, sound judgement.
- Jupiter w = Mars/Pluto m: unusual success.
- Jupiter w = Saturn/Moon's Node m: desire for seclusion, inner happiness due to sacrifices for others.

In summary we might say that these configurations make evident here the presence of a strong mutual attraction and the re-

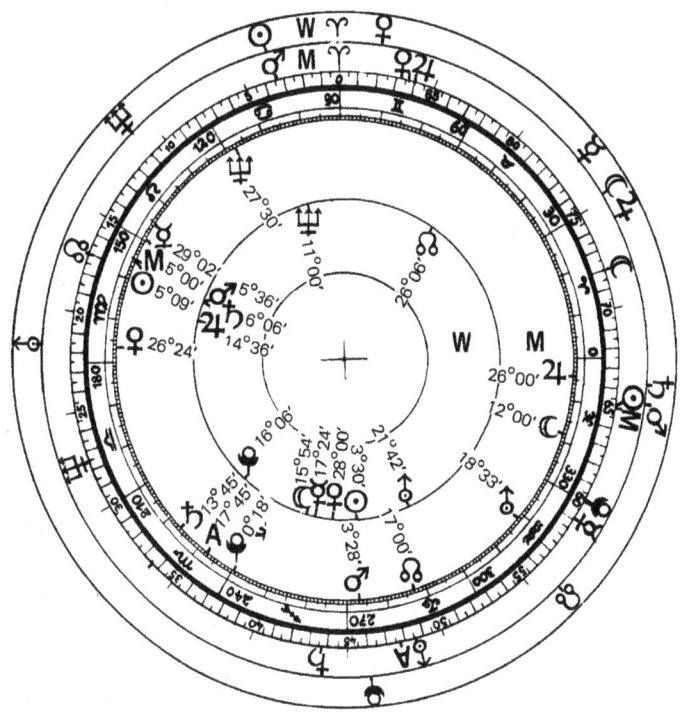

Figure 29
M = Goethe 28 Aug. 1749
W = Charlotte von Stein 25 Dec. 1742

ciprocation of constructive criticism, leading to joint successes and also to the repeated withdrawal of one from the other.

Since this relationship did have its tragic side, we see that Saturn w = Venus/Pluto w means tragic love which was suddenly ignited through Uranus w = Venus/Pluto w. This configuration coincides with Sun m and MC m, so that the man was at the root of the tragedy.

Now turning our attention to Mercury w, we see Mercury w = Sun/ Saturn w: occupation with serious problems.

- Mercury w = Sun/Mars w: readiness for action, realization of plans.
- Mercury w = Uranus/Pluto w: active mind, restless spirit, creativity, ingenuity.

Since Sun and Mars in both cosmograms mutually coincide, this makes it likely that the woman's intellect was a stimulation to the man's own thoughts and ideas (Sun/Mars).

In addition we find:

- Mercury w = Moon/Jupiter m: far-reaching plans, broad range of thought, goal-consciousness. Alliance with a rich or happy woman. Success through writing or the spoken word (CSI).
- Mercury w = Moon/Venus m: love's longing, reflecting on erotic problems.
- Mercury w = Uranus/Moon's Node m: quick grasp, united with others in thought, sudden mutual understanding (CSI).

All these configurations point to a deep friendship based on love, where each partner inspired and stimulated the other, but where, also, mutual reserves were maintained in order to avoid overstepping the boundaries set up by circumstance.

A third example will demonstrate what configurations result in a love tragedy.

Male nativity April 21, 1913, 8:00 p.m., Gardelegen (East Germany).
Female nativity April 10, 1920, 1:30 a.m., Kremkau (East Germany).

On October 27, 1935, at 5:00 p.m., the 22-year-old E.K. shot and killed the 15-year-old I.R. with whom he had been having an unhappy love affair. The fatally wounded girl died a half an hour after the shooting, her murderer died four weeks later in a mental hospital. The event itself has been discussed in full by Franz Hackbusch[13]. What we are primarily interested in is a synastry of the two natal charts.

The following configurations immediately strike the eye: MC w conjunction Moon m, AS m; Mars w opposition Venus m; Jupiter w with Neptune w square Venus m; Venus w square Pluto m.

Since instructions have already been given as to how to use the workboard, we might also dispense with a detailed investigation of the natal charts in the 360° circle, and we shall therefore concentrate primarily on the outer ring of the chart with the 90° graduation. We first adjust the calculating disc to point to MC w = AS m, because it is here that we may expect the strongest personal correlation.

The male natal chart shows:

- AS m = Mercury/Mars m: quarrelsome individual. AS m = Moon/Venus m: association with women, love relationship.
- AS m = Moon/Uranus m: excited individual, disquieting influence on others.
- AS m = Moon m: physical attraction.

This describes a quarrelsome and excitable individual who has a disquieting effect on others and who looks for relations with women.

The following configurations are to be found in the female chart:

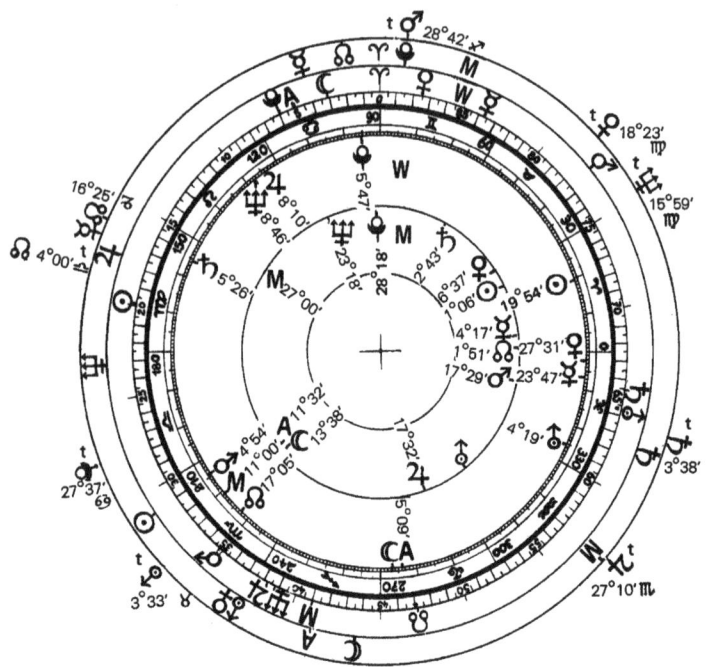

Figure 30
W= Ilse Rogengel, 10 April 1920
M = Ernst Klever, 21 April 1913

- MC w = Mars/Moon's Node w: sexual relationship.
  MC w = Sun/Uranus w: excitable, restless individual, emotional upset.
- MC w = Sun/Saturn w: inhibited development.
- MC w = Neptune w: lack of ego-consciousness.
- MC w = Jupiter w: goal-consciousness.
- MC w = Jupiter/Neptune w: harm through thoughtlessness.
- MC w = Mercury/Venus w: carelessness.

The girl is also excitable and restless, her development inhibited, she is imprudent and can suffer harm through inconsiderate action, seeks sexual relations.

The synastry m : w reveals:

- AS m = Mars/Moon's Node w: sexual relationship.
- AS m = Sun/Uranus w: sudden events.
- AS m = Sun/Saturn w: being misunderstood, separation.
- AS m = Neptune w: impressionability.
- AS m = Jupiter w: pleasant manners.
- AS m = Jupiter/Neptune w: living in a make-believe world.
- (AS m at 11° Scorpio does not form an exact square to the midpoint Jupiter/Neptune at 8° Leo, nevertheless the CSI combination of three interpretive factors may still be implemented.)
- AS m = Mercury/Venus w: thoughts of personal love.

Reversing to w : m we find:

- MC w = AS m: emotional and physical bond.
- MC w = Moon/Uranus m: readiness to act.
- MC w = Moon m: emotional and spiritual relationship.
- MC w = Moon/Venus m: to be satisfied by love.

According to the above, thoughts of love lead to mutual influence resulting in the beginning of a physical and emotional relationship, a sexual relationship therefore, without any awareness of the possible consequences (living in make-believe) bringing with it the danger of being misunderstood and a subsequent separation.

Let us now consider the Venus-Mars relationship. We find:

- Venus m = Uranus m: erotic excitement, amatory adventure.
- Venus m = Sun/AS m: affection.
- Uranus m = Sun/AS m: asserting oneself by force = Venus: in love (rape).
- Venus m = Sun/Moon m: erotic attraction.
- Uranus m = Sun/Moon m: sudden events in love-life.
- Venus m = Jupiter/MC m: wealth of amorous feeling.
- Uranus m = Jupiter/MC m: taking advantage of the right moment.
- Venus m = Mars/Pluto m: passionateness, rape.
- Uranus m = Mars/Pluto m: violence.
- Venus m = Mars/Jupiter w: harmonious sex-life. Uranus m = Mars/Jupiter w: rebelling against authority.
- Venus m = Mars/Neptune w: wrong ideas in love-life, abuse of pro-creative power.
- Uranus m = Mars/Neptune w: sudden disadvantages through lack of energy.
- Venus m = Mars w: love urge, passion. Venus m = Saturn/Pluto: alienation, desire to renounce love.
- Venus m = Saturn/AS w: inhibited love-life through environmental influences.
- Mars w = Sun/Moon's Node w: sexual union. Mars w = Uranus/Pluto w: violence, rashness.
- Mars w = Uranus/AS w: taking physical action, being threatened, harmed, injured.
- Mars w = Saturn/AS w: resisting suppression and restriction.
- Mars w = Venus m: love urge, passion.
- Mars w = Sun/Venus m: love impulse.
- Mars w = Sun/Uranus m: rash act, injury, mishap.

We see from all these configurations that the man sought to make use of the right opportunity in order to satisfy his desire for love, not even stopping short of violence. The girl rebel Is against any kind of domination, seeks sexual relations and runs into the danger of threat, injury and harm. The synastry also shows the joint impulse toward a sexual union. Both seem to act under false or obscure conceptions with the abuse of procreative powers.

The Venus-Pluto relationship involves the following combinations:

- Pluto m = Moon m: extremes in emotional life.
- Pluto m = Sun/MC m: achieving one's goals through force.
- Moon m = Sun/MC m: unconscious motivations, attitude to opposite sex.
- Venus w = Moon/Mercury w: feelings of love, youthful love.
- Venus w = Sun/Saturn w: inhibitions in love-life, love-sickness.
- Venus w = Sun/Uranus w: sudden love impulse, becoming quickly enamored, romantic or unusual love experience.
- Venus w = Mars/Moon's Node w: passionate union.
- Venus w = Jupiter/Moon's Node w: making oneself popular.
- Venus w = Neptune/Moon's Node w: false relations, having one's feelings disappointed by others.
- Pluto m = Venus w: fanatic love, lust.
- Pluto m = Moon/Mercury w: tragic perceptions.
- Moon m = Moon/Mercury w: thoughts guided by emotion.
- Moon m = Venus w: feelings of love, devotion.
- Pluto m = Sun/Saturn w: checks in development due to illness.

- Moon m = Sun/Saturn w: emotional depression, separation.
- Pluto m = Neptune/Moon's Node w: bad influence in relations, enervating relationship.
- Moon m = Neptune/Moon's Node w: disappointment, wrong kind of relationship to females.
- Venus w = Mercury/Mars m: quick determination in love matters, fight for the beloved woman.
- Venus w = Moon/AS m: love relationship, influence of the love union on personality.
- Venus w = Saturn/Neptune m: love suffering.

The square of Venus w and Pluto m in the synastry indicates in the man's case an emotional life ranging to extremes and unconscious impulses with regard to his attitude towards the opposite sex. and in the girl's case points to a sudden and very unusual love experience combined with the danger of disappointment, as well as to an incongruous relationship founded on lust, leading to tragic perceptions.

On investigating Mercury, it becomes very obvious that both individuals were not fully aware of their actions and that their thinking was subject to false or pathological conceptions.

- Mercury m = Mars/Neptune m: thoughtlessness, feeble-mindedness.
- Mercury m = Venus/Saturn m: strait-laced or selfish in love.
- Mercury m = Saturn/Uranus m: placing great demands on nerve potential.
- Mercury m = AS/MC m: reflections on one's own self.
- Mercury w = Jupiter/Neptune w: active imagination, to give rise to hopes, play-acting.
- Mercury w = Neptune w: disturbances coming from the

subconscious.
- Mercury w = Neptune w = Mars/MC w: acting rashly and falsely.
- Mercury m = Moon/AS w: seeking to establish personal contact.
- Mercury m = Moon/Pluto w: exercising a great influence on others.
- Mercury m = Mars/Saturn w:thoughtlessness,hopelessness, thoughts on separation and death. Murderer. (In the CSI the word "murderer" is given in parentheses, because, for obvious reasons, this interpretation will not be applicable in every case, but there are indications here of a premeditated murder, especially since Mercury m is aligned with the personal points Moon and AS w.)
- Mercury m = Mars/Uranus w: a calculated test of nerves, a well-thought-out achievement, injury, nervous strain.
- Mercury m = AS/Pluto w: attempt to dominate others mentally, the power of suggestion, hypnosis.

According to the above, the man exercised a demonical influence on the girl; his ideas were enhanced by violence and brutality and ended in murder. Here we take note of the fact that Mercury is in almost every case involved in a direct midpoint.

Setting up the two natal charts separately, it strikes us that in both cases the Moon is located on the Ascendant, in the girl's case Pluto and in the man's case Sun with Venus are on the Descendant, endowing the horizontal axis with special significance, in connection with the man's Mercury position in relation to Mars/Saturn and Mars/Uranus in the girl's chart, from which the planned rape and the subsequent murder can also be derived.

- Mercury w = Neptune w = Mars/Pluto m: nervous strain, maliciousness, secret harm.
- Mercury w = Neptune w = Venus/AS m: exchange of love thoughts, immoral behavior, falseness, disappointment.
- Mercury w = Neptune w = Uranus/AS m: expressing criticism, suffering emotionally and mentally because of restless persons, disappointment, falseness, sudden undermining of relations, sudden sad experience.
- Mercury w = Neptune/MC m: misguided thinking, wrong ideas, the emergence of unconscious notions.

Even if we investigate other planetary pictures, the result is always the same. Writing down the various events in keywords, we obtain a clear-cut picture of the tragedy:

The man: pugnacious, restless, excitable, passionate with perverse inclinations, violent, capable of committing rape, neurotic, imbecile, frequently acting without full awareness of the real situation.

The girl: excitable, restless, careless, thoughtless, passionate, acting under obscure conceptions, willing for an unusual love experience with the potential danger of seduction and rape.

The relationship: urge for physical-emotional union, lustful desire, rape, abuse of procreative power, incongruous relationship, tragic perceptions, danger of separation through death by violence.

The following configurations typify the day of the murder (October 27, 1935):

- Uranus t 3° 31' Taurus = Sun t 3°21' Scorpio = Moon 4°28' Scorpio (New Moon) = Mars w 4° 54' Scorpio =

Moon/Saturn w = Uranus/ AS w = Uranus/Pluto w = Sun/Moon's Node w, from which we may conclude violence, injury or even murder. These axes coincide with Mars m = Mercury/Saturn: doing harm to others, bringing about separation by force (CSI).
- Mars t 29° 04' Sagittarius has just passed over opposition Pluto m, semisquare Moon m and square Venus w and hence triggers the critical .Venus-Pluto aspect. Oddly enough, Saturn appears in all cosmograms in the same axis, viz. Saturn t 3°37' Pisces. Saturn m 2°47' Gemini, Saturn w 5°26' Virgo, again aspecting here Uranus w. Sun w, Venus/MC w, Pluto/AS w etc.

To make reading easier, the individual aspects have not always been named, instead the equal sign was given to mean, as the case may be, conjunction, semisquare, square, sesquiquadrate, and opposition. There are many schools of thought rejecting the designation of the 45°, 90° and 135° angles to the midpoints as indirect planetary pictures, but experience has repeatedly shown that these may indeed be implemented, using, however, a small orb.

The last example was intended to show how by using the work-board and the CSI a quick overall view comprising precise interpretations can be obtained, if one does take the trouble to investigate really all of the aspects of the interpretive factors. Of course, it would actually have also been necessary to consider the positions of the stellar bodies in the individual signs of the zodiac, in the last example, for instance these were Venus m in Taurus opposition Mars w in Scorpio, Venus w in Pisces square Pluto m in Gemini, etc. However, an all-encompassing investigation such as that would on its own have filled an entire book. The purpose of this discussion was to give impetus to careful and precise investigations and work based on a true sense of responsibility, especially important in the field of comparative analysis in order, in these times of rampant marital crisis, to give forewarnings of precipancy and rashness with regard to marrying, to uncover potential dangers to a marriage, and to promote mutual understanding. If this book should prove to be of use in marriage counseling in this way, then it will have served its purpose. By no means, however, should the advice of psychologists and physicians be disregarded, for it is only on this foundation, utilizing the psychological, medical and cosmobiological knowledge of a mature and experienced man, that marriage counseling can be of use.

References

1. Reinhold Ebertin, *Charakter und Schicksal im Kosmogramm*, Aalen, 1950. (This book is out of print; in its stead please confer *Man in the Universe* and *Der Mensch und sein Gestirn*.)
2. Ernst Kretschmer, *Körperbau und Charakter*. Heidelberg 1948.
3. C.G. Jung, *Psychologische Typen*, Zurich 1925.
4. Manfred Curry, *Der Schlüssel zum Leben*, Zurich 1949.
5. Reinhold Ebertin, *Kosmopsychologie*, Aalen 1950/1966.
6. Dr. Ernst Speer, *Die Liebesfähigkeit des Menschen*, Münchon 1951.
7. Reinhold Ebertin. CSI, *The Combination of Stellar Influences*, Aalen 1950/1972.
8. Reinhold Ebertin, *Direktionen*, Aalen 1966.
9. Carter, *Aspekte*, München 1938.
10. Elsbeth Ebertin, *Astrologie und Liebesleben*, Görlitz 1926.
11. Parm, *Individualformen, Kosmobiolog*. Kartei, Aalen 1951.
12. Reinhold Ebertin, *The 90° Workboard in Cosmobiological Practice, cf. Applied Cosmobiology*, Aalen 1970.
13. Dr. H.H. Kritzinger, *Todesstrahlen und Wünschelrute*, Leipzig 1929.
14. Franz, Hackbusch. *Tragisches Ende einer jungen* Liebe, Mensch im All, Juni 1936.

Abbreviations

m = male
w = female
t = transiting
p = progressive
CSI = Combination of Stellar Influences

www.ingramcontent.com/pod-product-compliance
Ingram Content Group UK Ltd.
Pitfield, Milton Keynes, MK11 3LW, UK
UKHW041422180426
11947UKWH00007B/244